Lost
Kings and Queens

Albernithy

Thank you for supporting my vision

KEEP Ruling "Queen"

Finding Our Lost Kings and Queens

Strategies for Empowering Our Future Kings & Queens

Jay Barnett

Finding Our Lost Kings and Queens: Strategies for Empowering Our Lost Kings & Queens
©2013 by Jay Barnett

Cover photo and design by Tawana Cox of ETC Studios:
www.etcstudios.net
Text design by Lisa DeSpain of www.ebookconverting.com

Dedication

I would like to dedicate this book to the one who gives me strength when I'm weak. My lord and savior Jesus Christ, I praise God for giving me a chance to tell my story. I am so humbly blessed, to have a vision that will empower people around the world. I do not take it lightly. I cherish every opportunity given to share my message. None of this would be possible if it weren't for the two greatest people in my life, my parents. I dedicate this book to my awesome dad, King Jimmy Barnett Sr. I love you more than you know, Dad. I am so very proud to be your son. To my beautiful mother Queen Mary: every morning I wake up I hear your voice, saying don't quit and that I AM A KING. Mama, you called me a king even when I had a servant mentality. I thank you for that. I love you dearly Mama, I am so blessed to have a mother like you. Also, I dedicate this book to my Angels Candrease and Priscilla: a brother could not have asked for better sisters. I am very grateful for the days you girls have been my strength. To my nieces Kyliegh and Aleyah: remain queens, and know that Jay will always love his Angels.

Table of Contents

Faded Dream
For A Clear Vision

*J*ust as sail boats drift into the open sea, my dreams to become a professional athlete did as well. Shaped and molded for heavy lifting and excruciating conditioning along with eating regimens that never seemed to curb my appetite, I ate, slept, and breathed football. There was always a lot of "not enough" conversations; you're not big enough—lift more; you're not fast enough—get faster; and the one that no man can control—height, you're not tall enough. Every opposition was my opportunity to prove people wrong. So the conversations fueled my tank. It may have been easier to quit rather than to deal with the harsh criticism of the sport. But quitting was not an option.

Yet, I was an 'I can show you better than I can tell you' guy. I went against the grain; I cut against the pattern that was laid out before me for the pursuit of my humanly value. I was bred from a family of strong and athletic men that declared their popularity through being the town's greatest. Little did I know, my path would be modified for a different purpose. My dad had made a name for himself as one of the town greatest football players. He began a legacy in which an uncle and two cousins would follow, and in turn lead them to the NFL. At times, I felt pressure to live up to the expectations. "Be better than dad in everything" was my life mission statement. I *wasn't driven by the family legacy. My fire was burning from something deeper within. My motivation was induced through bitterness and resentment toward my father. I would sleep to ease my pain, and dreaming created a world that I wished to live in. At times I would think that my dream was a nightmare and if I could just wake up, all would be great.*

It wasn't all bad. I had an awesome high school career, but it was short lived and followed by a nightmare of not graduating high school because of my inadequacy for test taking. All my hurt and pain fueled my sleep so I could continue to dream about showing people that I was good enough. The first out of five children to go to college, I didn't know I was setting a standard that was never expected to be set. Many of my family members thought I would fall victim to the streets and to the dysfunctional family excuse that many use. What they didn't know was that I loved to sleep, because I could dream for hours and hours of being a success.

I loved to sleep, because I could dream for hours and hours of being a success.

College was such a blur; it didn't feel like I had spent four years of my life wearing purple & white. Many times my emotions and pain were often provoked through my mom's problems. In some cases this worked in my favor because I could live for her on the field, because I felt free. Pain made me a beast; my past brought my Frankenstein to life, while my hurt whispered in my ear daily. I would walk away as the university's first four year starter still feeling empty inside. My life had transitioned to the dreams I had of becoming a professional athlete, yet never did I imagine my dream would fade.

Undrafted, the Philadelphia Eagles changed their mind about a free agent deal. The Pittsburg Steelers said I wasn't big enough to ride the back seat of the BUS (Jerome Bettis).

There I was, left with uncertainties, dreams, and hope. Finally, a call came from the Green Bay Packers. After going up to Green Bay and experiencing what I thought would be a childhood dream come true, all I was left with was a faded dream. I possessed all the right tools, but my toolbox was not needed for the job. I am forever grateful for the opportunity given by the Packers. I will always be a "cheese head" in my heart. But it's hard to forget a broken promise. The pursuit of being the "next one" slowly diminished as thoughts of being a FAILURE began to emerge. A failure is what I was; at least that is what I thought. Chasing the family legacy into the NFL had faded without my consent. Sleeping was common now because I did not want to wake up from this dream. Reality walked into my room and stood over my bed and began to whisper; the more he whispered the more my dream began to fade. I could hear his voice calling my name but I refused to wake up.

The images no longer looked vivid, they began to become dim and dimmer. Finally, I had awakened to grief, sorrow, and the voices of the antagonistic groups I had acquired. I was left in a room with my thoughts and a knife that would decide my fate forever. Suicide had become a friend that I often entertained because he would always come with a solution to the problem.

A faded dream had caused me to never want to sleep again because I could no longer dream what I wanted. Reaching out towards life after death became a regular conversation of mine.

Death appeared in the room and said, "I think it's time we stop talking and let's finish this."

But then God intervened and said, "I cannot stop you from taking your life, it is your choice. But I can help only if YOU decide to live."

Tears streaming down my face and a knife pressed against my wrist, I wasn't interested in what God had to say. Death had convinced me that suicide was the best option. I opened my ears, but with a closed mind.

God continued to speak, and the more He spoke, death continued as well. "I can't stop you but I can help you, Jay."

God said, "You must decide to live."

Death said, "Live for what? You have failed and there is nothing else you can do."

So, I asked, "Help me understand. Why didn't I make it?"

God said "I allowed your dream to fade so I could make your vision clear. Your vision will take you places your dreams could not."

I don't sleep anymore because I have restrictions on dreaming. Therefore my eyes are wide open so I can see my vision.

My story in short… Jay Barnett

Preface

*H*ow does one find something that they didn't even know was lost? What significance does it hold if no one even knew it could be found? Sometimes there is a point in life when things are discovered without ever searching for them.

Losing something that once was of great importance in your life can lead to immense frustration when it's not recovered. What if that something was more than a possession? What if it was a part of your soul? Many have lost their place in society, living day to day, holding on by a string, and praying that tomorrow will bring just enough hope to continue on. Some have never possessed anything only to realize that they were lost in life. Some, unfortunately, pray the next day is their last. These are the individuals that are among OUR lost.

How is it that tribe after tribe, generation after generation, family after family, can continue a cycle of being misplaced to never be found? Just as mathematicians search for the missing number that completes the equation and scientist's research the unknown, why is it that we, as people, don't seek?

Those that are lost can't always find themselves, and don't always recognize that they are lost. However, each and every one of us can be seekers of the lost, yet very few of us do. Some don't know how or where to seek them out and others just don't want to be bothered.

Our next generation of leaders has been taken by a series of distractions. With all the new technology at our fingertips—social media, mass media access, cell phones/texting—we have socially handicapped many of our youth for the next phase of their lives. The art and the importance of actual human interaction has been lost in the airwaves. There is far less verbal communication, and no real interaction within the school setting, peer to peer, or parents to kids.

Moving quickly and seeking instant gratification are the motivators of today's culture and the downfall of our society. "Speed kills," according to all my football coaches. In the process of moving quickly, whatever is lost during the transition from point A to point B is usually lost forever—never to be found. At the same time, what was missed in the high speed transition will never missed, because no one ever acknowledged it or saw any purpose in it. This is what is happening to our younger generation. We are moving along so quickly in life that we don't take the time to see what we have overlooked in the parenting and education of our children. There is far too much housing of our youth and way too little parenting. We pacify our youth with electronics rather than stopping to actually listen to them.

In the past there were lost youth, struggling to figure out where they fit in. But nowadays, the percentage of youth that is lost has increased drastically to the point where child suicide, drug addiction, pregnancy, and criminal records have become common. All these lost youth have the makings to be a king or a queen. They were born kings and queens but along the way someone lost their crown and birth rights. Until we find our missing, unacknowledged kings and queens, the generations to come will be raised by those already lost. They will repeat the cycle, adding even more lost to the world.

A king inherits responsibility through family order; in most cases the son takes over at the time of death or if the king is deemed unfit to rule. At birth, the heirs to the throne are anointed with a royal destiny. This has been chosen before he or she even knows of a thing called free will. A royal mentality is instilled at the early stages of childhood. Each child born in this world is a king or queen in the making. They are all born with a royal destiny. It is a God-given right. It is up to us to make sure they reach their full potential, to ensure they do not become a statistic—one of the lost.

They were born kings and queens but along the way someone lost their crown and birth rights.

Chapter 1
Undeveloped Kings

My parents divorced when I was 13 years old. This is a time I consider to be a pivotal year for many young men. These should have been my developmental years; the years when I would develop my work habits, behavior patterns, and form opinions based on my experiences. Because of the separation of my parents, I became undeveloped in a lot of different areas. This can be attributed to the fact that I was forced into manhood far too soon due to my father turning in his resignation papers.

This timeframe where I needed support to grow and experience were crucial to me and my future, yet I stood it alone. I was required to take charge of a position that I knew nothing about, which was being the man of the house. Becoming a man so soon worked against me. I was not prepared or coached for this position. Becoming a father figure and husband all in one day would be the story of my teenage years.

There are so many other undeveloped young men because life happens; they had to step up because a dad or someone else chose to step down. The life skills we should have learned by now did not occur—rather they were forced upon us.

It wasn't until I got much older and was able to look back over my life that I observed the patterns of my behavior and realized why I wasn't progressing. I was unlearned, unskilled, and undeveloped due to invalid teachings. Because of this I had to teach myself later in life the things that were left untaught.

Is this the issue with the majority of men on the earth? Some may have become teenage fathers, fathers by default, or in some cases, fathers that weren't fathered. Because of the lack of structure or a role model, those who come from these situations tend to suffer the most. Then the youth that follow these undeveloped kings suffer too. It is a vicious cycle. Until the strategies and methods to develop the undeveloped and provide them with the skills they need to become better fathers and father figures, the cycle will continue.

The result of me not knowing proper life skills had a negative effect on my life in so many areas. I was undeveloped in my youth, and mentored by undeveloped men. If you are an unfinished product, how can you finish another product?

Society has made it acceptable for men to walk away from their responsibility. This results in a domino effect, destroying so many other things around it. Being raised in a situation where not finishing is the norm creates a mentality among children that quitting, doubting oneself, complaining and becoming slothful is an acceptable form of behavior.

So many kings are not being developed properly, either their fathers have disappeared or the necessary skills haven't been taught. Not having these proper skills to become a good father results in their children turning out the same. Passing down the same behavioral patterns and negative thinking that has led to part of the corruption in our society. Sadly, this in turn has led to the acceptance by society for a woman to have a family, but not have a man properly involved.

One of the worst things that can happen is to have lost kings passing down a servant's attitude. Although I do believe there is a time and a place for the attitude of serving, one cannot learn to control or govern something if they were only taught a servants' mentality. The value of procreation has diminished. It is males creating babies, not kings creating heirs. Any irresponsible, unmotivated male can lay with a female and make a baby, but it takes a responsible, structured, developed man to raise and develop a king.

So many youth are forced to learn the hard way as they go through life, right or wrong, the necessary life skills to be a parent. This is what leads to so many parents passing down the same behavior that they experienced while growing up. Unless one seeks the necessary help or proper education needed to become an adequate role model fit to rear our future kings and queens, they will produce more lost youth.

The Disney movie *The Lion King* shows a great example of instilling the proper mindset in one's offspring. King Mufasa, Simba's dad in *The Lion King,* instilled in Simba the knowledge and desire to become a king one day. Helping a child understand the process in becoming a king is something that only a king can pass down through his wisdom and knowledge. Teaching him that having power comes with responsibility and that one should not abuse that power simply to get what they want is a valuable lesson.

Some are taught that power equals control and the ability to manipulate others. Some believe power provides us with the opportunity to do as we wish. Those who preach this nonsense are undeveloped. This is just one of the many false principles that we are taught as young men.

Back to *The Lion King*—what Mufasa taught Simba prepared him for the day that his dad would no longer be in existence. He was developed to the point where he could manage what he gained and not lose what he was given, which was his Kingship. Ruling a kingdom is never an easy process. The foundation his father built was diminishing. Simba realized he was trained to rule. But if one does not know they were created to rule, they will be ruled by something or someone. This is how gangs and other forms of negativity have been able to control the path of so many young kings. They have no idea who or what they are supposed to be. There are far too few examples of Mufasa in society today. Rather, we have false kings posing as dope dealers, athletes, or music entertainers with a false pretense of a king.

Most of these so called role models are undeveloped themselves. They tend to hide behind the helmet, the dunks and the music, presenting to everyone that they are happy and leading a full and productive life. As I was forced to grow and recognize my inadequacies, I too needed to finish the development process and recognize where I needed to grow. I have learned this through years of developing and changing the old behaviors I adopted. If you don't know you are destined for greatness, you can never obtain it. How can these younger kings that we seek be effective without being educated?

If one does not know he was created to rule, he will be ruled by something or someone.

They will not become a menace to society as the system states; they will become a menace to themselves. One day they will awaken, like myself, and may dislike what they have been taught.

Your Past Can Affect Your Development...

Until you face the music, you will never accept full responsibility for your actions. Unless you face past failures and hurt, you will not be able to move past them. The pattern of not properly developing the lost will continue to proceed on a road that has a dead end. I carried the hurt of my parent's divorce for over 10 years. I was mad and upset at my father because I yearned for his mentorship and the opportunity to learn from him. I wanted to learn the process of being a man; I sought for his teachings, skill set, and the things that could help prepare me to rule just as Mufasa did for Simba. I carried malice and resentment towards him for years which I allowed to grow into HATE, which was very ugly.

But one day I heard God's voice speak to my heart and say "The longer you carry this hate and resentment, the longer you will struggle."

I responded, "I hear you God, I hear you, but what he has done has affected me as a man today."

God replied, "I know it did, but are you perfect?"

I broke down because I knew in my heart that my father was a great man, he and my mother just didn't work out. What I learned from that revelation was who was I to judge or hold this grudge? I knew I wasn't perfect. The longer I maintained that attitude, I realized that I was the one who was holding up my own development. I sat down and wrote my dad a letter and let him know that I forgave him and that I was willing to move forward with our relationship and start anew. Writing that letter would soon reveal things I didn't know about myself.

Reading some of this may force you to confront your past, people that have hurt you, or confront a past experience that is currently affecting your development. The reason the past affects us so much is because it tends to cripple us for the future. If I never found the courage to face my past, I wouldn't be able to face other kings and help develop them because I myself would be still undeveloped.

We all have our issues, but we have to confront them so that past issues do not rear their ugly head and confront us later in life. Our youth is searching out guidance because we are not stepping up to the plate to give it to them. In turn, they look to the television, music, drugs, gangs, etc. as their mentors and leaders. This is why we have to confront the past so there is no interference with the teachings that we pass down from one generation to the next. Clear instructions and wisdom are the keys that can unlock any door. The bible says that in all of your getting's, you should also get an understanding of the circumstances. Some of us may get, but we don't get an understanding.

Understand and know that your past will come up in the present which will affect the future, not just for you but for everyone else in your life as well. We ourselves need to develop the right mindset if we are ever going to turn this crisis amongst our youth around.

13 And Angry...

The coming of another phase in life is very interesting, especially when it comes faster than the human mind can keep up with. Like most teens, their body outgrows the mind, constantly playing catch up. I was filled with questions and had no answers; left in the dark with no flashlight with an untamed beast. Finally as a teenager, I had grown up with an attitude and opinion that disputed everything and everyone around me. I had bark with a bite and was a ticking time bomb, filled with a venom called pain. As an adolescent, my worst nightmare had become my reality all too soon.

My dad walked out after 15 years of marriage, the shock of my first year of puberty. The man that I once rubbed nose to nose with, who told me he loved me, would exit with no regards. Unbelievable, despicable, and unimaginable were words that I came to use often during this nightmare.

The year I was looking forward to having my dad support me in junior high would be dismissed due to his act of quitting. A monster would be created within my heart and mind. Getting kicked out of class and disrupting teachers in mid-sentence was an act of kindness. Fighting girls and looking for a challenge from the baddest kid in school was a daily thing. I wanted to make someone pay; I was hurting, therefore somebody had to be on the receiving end. Junior high was a lab within my mind; I could test and use any dose of anger I had stored inside. I didn't care. I didn't give a damn about anything. The very man I had once respected became a joke that I wanted to tell everyone so I could laugh to hide my inner pain.

I carried my anger around like a red wagon filled with toys, but my toys were a set of dumbbells that my dad once bought me. Bench pressing him and physically throwing him became a visual that I looked forward to living. Only time would tell if I could test the old man. My anger had driven me by the room he stayed in because he stopped sleeping in the same room as my mother.

Like a bully looking for lunch money, I was waiting for him to discipline me about my chores. I ignored and disrespected his authority of being my dad. This was my moment to test the bench press move; I voiced my opinion as if I were speaking through a mega phone. "You can't tell me what to do and I don't respect you" was my statement. The ranting began *just as I imagined. Yes, yes, yes! Do something! I pushed him and he pushed back harder, my training had upheld its end of the bargain; I didn't fall down. The shoving was fueled even more by my anger. My anger stemmed from his abandonment of his son.*

The match ended in a draw with the interference of my mother. I had an attitude because I no longer felt like my own father was worth my time. He left, but I was going to show him that I could be a man without him.

Driven by my anger and lead by pain was the story of my teen years. Everyone was the enemy including my aunts and uncles because I felt they all had a sense of what was happening.

A scholar student all my life; please!!! My education was vengeance 101. It was an open class that whoever attended could learn. Unlike many teachers, my test was an open book with a curriculum built on disappointment and resentment.

Football became very dear to me. Finally I had found a way to unleash my anger without repercussion. This is awesome, I thought; I could finally unleash the beast that was created. I could punish, and possibly kill my opponent. I became a menace to myself, as well as society. Once during a game, I could sense the fear of the kid across from me. It may have been fun for him at first, until he was later left with a broken collarbone. For me it was revenge and I was the HULK with a helmet. My anger had driven me to the edge, and left me feeling no remorse. It became a joke to me. I made my presence known that I was not the kid to cross; I was not very big but I packed an attitude of a monster that would eat you and spit you out.

Yes my dad created this mess, is what I thought. If you don't like it, call and tell him to come back home. It's too late and I had already swallowed the poison. Happy years they should had been; instead 13 was the year that I would birth the mind of an unpredictable boy that was hurting. Anger was my breakfast. Hatred filled me at lunch. I snacked on bitterness, and for dinner, vengeance was served. When I used the restroom, I released out the pain that was caused by absorbing all of this garbage. It's amazing what a broken family can do to a kid. I lived it; 13 and angry.

Chapter 2
Why Are They Lost?

Contrary to what we may want to hear, think, or believe, our lost youth are in plain sight. They are the youth that will be running our nation—the upcoming generation. They are in the schools, they are in your neighborhood, they can be your neighbor's child, and they might even be your own child. They come in all colors, sizes, cultures, and economic backgrounds. It was once me and it could have been you as well. Their future was destined to be bright, but somewhere along the way, that bulb began to flicker and was never replaced. They became a statistic—one of our many lost kings and queens.

Why are they lost? Numerous factors play into the reason so many of our youth are falling to the wayside. Single parent households are one of the common denominators with many lost children. It is becoming the new norm as well as a silent crisis that is creating less emotionally fit youth. One out of every four households is supported by a single parent. According to the 2011 US Census Bureau, 11.7 million families in the US were headed by a single parent, 85.2% of which were headed by a female. Around 55% of these single parent households were created through divorce, separation, or widowed. The divorce rate is currently running at 50%. This doesn't even include all the children who were born to single mothers who never married.

For every divorce involving children, the odds of another lost child rises. In 2010, the United States population was 308,745,538. Out of that number, 2,096,000 people were married and out of the total population 872,000 individuals got divorced or an annulment.

When getting a divorce has become easier than getting a driver license, there is a problem. Couples are getting divorces for reasons as weak as someone "got bored" in the relationship. The reasons behind marriage and the sacredness of the vows are lost in today's masses. Divorce is now the quick fix for those who do not want to put the work into what a marriage entails. Many people are going into marriage with the mentality that if it doesn't work out or feel right for whatever reason they can always just get a divorce. What does this teach our youth?

In 2011, there were 2.3 million mothers with children under 18 years of age who were unemployed, according to a recent report from the Labor Department. Single mothers account for more than half—1.2 million—of the total number of unemployed mothers. Half of single mother families have an annual income less than $25,000. Only one third of these single mothers receive any child support, and the average amount these mothers receive is only about $300 a month. (Catalyst.org, April 2012) Two thirds of all single mothers receive food stamps. Among children with single mothers, 41% get food stamps and the remaining get nothing.

Lower educated parents also contribute to the lost children statistics. With a lower educational background, or if the parent had poor school performance, more times than not their income levels are just as poor, leading to extra stress when children come into the picture. Stress and depression due to poverty situations can lead to self-medication with illegal drugs and alcohol because professional help is thought to be unattainable or shunned due to lack of knowledge about the services. Depressed parents raise depressed children, which adds to our lost population.

Single parent homes are not the only reason many of our youth are lost. They can come from a married household as well. With the cost of living and people wanting to live in the fast lanes, many married couples with children are finding that both parents have to work full time jobs, oftentimes with one picking up an additional part time job. This leaves a lot of unsupervised free time in a child's hands. It also takes away a lot of communication and interaction time with a child that is essential to healthy, emotional growth. It can leave many children feeling neglected, no matter what tokens parents are giving them to pacify them and relieve parental guilt for their lack of sufficient parenting. This too creates a lost child.

Other factors that play a huge role in creating our lost regardless of marital status is lack of parenting skills and simply immature parents. More and more children are being born to our youth—youth that have no clue as to what it takes to raise their child(ren).

Abuse plays another huge factor in the creation of lost youth. Abuse is not just beating your child. Abuse is also neglect, sexual, physical, mental, or verbal in nature. When a child endures one or more of these abusive behaviors you can count on them becoming lost if they do not receive any help and support.

The reaction to this is that we are losing our youth due to the deficiency of parenting, teaching, and mentoring. It can start in the home and sadly be carried through into a child's outside environment. The child can appear disobedient, withdrawn, a goof off, or even like any other child peer—masking what they are really feeling by trying to act the "norm". Their behavior outside the home affects their school performance and peer interaction, resulting in school officials pushing them to the side to concentrate on those students they deem worthy of their attention.

Where are the lost? They are everywhere! Some are home alone when not in school, often on weekends, and sometimes even into the late hours of the night and early mornings while the parent(s) is having "me" time. Most are greeted with takeout instead of a home cooked meal, and are rarely acknowledged or shown the slightest concern of how their day was. The lost are often barked orders rather than given any form of routine and structure. Their inaccurate verbal skills are due to the fact that the parent would rather text than talk, or "talk at" rather than "talk to" their child. Then you have kids who babysit their younger siblings, while managing household chores due to the absence of a responsible adult. These are the children that are handling adult situations with a child's mentality—they are being forced to grow up far too fast. They are their own parents.

Our lost youth are functionally illiterate students who stroll from grade to grade, never to comprehend the lessons that are taught. A large majority of students receive little or no guidance at all, but are expected to be the best. They're jocks on the field, but flunkies in the classroom. There are a few students ready and eager to learn but a teacher must appear. Our society is failing in education as well as educating. We are the teachers—from the parents to the educators—from the priest to the pastor, from the police officer to mentors, aunts, uncles, friends, and yes, sometimes even a complete stranger. We're all responsible for our lost kings and queens.

Chapter 3
Mentality Of Today's Youth

Back in the day there was a different level of respect a child had towards adult figures in their life. There was an unspoken respect and honor. Today, that type of respect is lacking in our youth and quite frankly, the fault for this lies with us adults. We have become a society too busy to slow down long enough to even acknowledge there is a fatal epidemic going on with our youth. Adults have a huge responsibility in how our youth's minds are developed, but at times we are failing them.

Media has a huge influence on our youth, and when you mix that with lack of supervision and guidance, the mentality of our youth is deteriorating drastically. Our youth is swallowed by the media's pressure of having swagg at all costs—to where our youth are willing to do anything and everything to be the fly'ist kid. They are intimated by the intelligent because they feel inferior; therefore the lost are pushed aside—neglected and often rejected with many left plotting their suicide. They find guidance in lyrics that even a deaf man could hear the corruption it has to offer.

It is my personal belief that homosexuality is who you are from birth. But this generation has no sense of identity; they experiment without taking precautions. It has become a game to some to be promiscuous. They are confused about who they want to become and who they are entirely. Society has opened Pandora's box and it's hard to close, because nothing is taboo. Anything goes. However, your sexuality is a choice. There is a problem when someone is influenced by media because it's the new thing. This is one issue that can lead youth into a spiral of self-destruction. It becomes an issue beyond sexual identity; it now it becomes an identity crisis.

Our lost youth's mentality is in the dark corners covered in black, on the sidewalks with indecent exposure because sagging is a fashion statement. They are attracted to sex with multiple partners, highlighted for hosting rainbow parties, a party where female lines up 5-10 guys and perform oral sex on each guy with a different color lipstick. They are infected with STD'S and AIDS at a higher rate than ever before.

Schools have become the playing field for retaliation of the hurt, and open season for the outcast. Gun alert drills have become just as common as fire drills. Teachers have given up, and put down their chalk, only for our officers to pick up that chalk and draw body outlines in the street. Our youth are creating story lines for mainstream media, giving screenplay writers new material daily. Violence is steadily rising and crimes are committed without remorse. Is this the mentality we want our children to have? If it isn't your child's mentality, count yourself blessed, but be aware, a child with this mentality may sit next to yours.

Students are in school bathrooms soaking tampons in alcohol so that it absorbs faster than a speeding bullet. One can only wish they were simply smoking cigarettes to rebel; instead they are sniffing bath salt to get high. Some ride around all day smoking weed, and inhaling whatever they can get their hands on, not realizing the long term effects or caring.

They are hiding in their bedrooms because of the school bully, the same bully who doesn't like the fact they can see themselves in their victims. They find themselves sitting on the edge of their bed with a loaded gun, contemplating pulling the trigger. Suicide is the 3rd leading cause of death for teens. 1 out of every 5 students in the schools today has considered suicide and 1 out of every 10 have made serious plans to do so. These numbers are alarming, and we as adults are responsible for stepping up and taking active measures to connect with our youth to stop this tragedy.

Our lost kings and queens are crying for help, but we are too busy with our own issues. So they become harder and tougher and far more evasive making them next to impossible to find if we are not even looking. Rather than having family dinners they are joining gangs for the brotherhood and bond of the false display of family. Their fists are filled with anger, eager to retaliate for the pain that has been brought on to them by others.

The lost king fights with the teacher and punches the kid who has said he is gay. He knows nothing about being a man except for what he sees on television and what he hears on the radio. The lost queen looks for love in all the wrong places. She finds herself in the arms of a teacher, a neighbor, or any male figure who gives her attention, compromising her innocence with their lack of morals. The lost kings and lost queens are feeling void from the world; the outside becomes the enemy and the inside becomes the friend that only exists in their imaginations.

We have been quiet when it matters the most and vocal when it doesn't. Too long we have let television, music, drugs, and the media take hold of our youth keeping them from their crown. A crown is fitted for a king that knows he is fit to be a king. The same goes for queens; her crown is not her value, it is a representation of her place in the royal palace. Until we demand our lost kings and queens be rescued, their kingdom will continue to collapse. This is something we cannot be silent about. We must speak up!

Troubled youth are lost because of lack of guidance. We have looked the other way for our own selfish reasons. We have chosen not to seek them out and lift them up; instead we leave them to their own devices to problem solve—which unfortunately is in all the wrong places.

One can only emulate what they see, if you want to change your view, then change what you are looking at. This is what needs to be accomplished with our youth. We need to embody what we want them to strive for. Our environment has produced a product that is reproducing rapidly—that product being our ever increasing inventory of lost kings and queens.

These behaviors and many more that are stealing our youth can be turned around, but it does require that everyone be proactive. It takes work, and it takes the willingness to reach out to the lost kings and queens. Have we become so self-indulged with our own success that we have created a gap between us and our youth that no one is willing to close? Society has deceived us into believing more is better, when in fact better is when we understand that more is not worth the sacrifice of losing our kings and queens in the making.

Chapter 4
Today's King

Merriam-Webster defines a king as "a male monarch of a major territorial unit, one whose position is hereditary and who rules for life; one that holds preeminent position; especially, a chief among competitors." This is a profound definition of what a king is or what a king should be. I find it in the game of strategy: Chess. The king is the most important piece, giving it the power to move in any direction and capture opposing pieces. But if someone is playing the game of chess, and does not know the power of the king, they will get checkmated in a very short time. A king can move at any angle, but he is limited if he is not protected by his queen. He can control the game at his own discretion, obtaining whatever he desires. If the piece is there and he wants it, he can take it. All of this takes critical thinking, in which a lot of our young kings lack. The same as the board game, our life works in a similar way. We must learn strategy, precision, and understand it is a process to rule. But, our young kings must be taught they can rule their territory before doing so.

Today's youth have created a totally different meaning for the word "king." A king is not someone who eats grapes and rides around merrily in his royal wagon. The vision of a king today in our youths' minds is one who is draped in Gucci and Louis Vuitton, with a belt laced in diamonds.

This king has earned his crown through street credibility and lyrics he exaggerated in the studio.

Yes, this is the meaning of a king in today's society, he controls his environment with mix tapes that flood the streets with vigorous sounds of how to get money at all costs. Then you have the king of the courts; he can add up all the points he scored, but can't add the millions he's lost. Who has crowned them? We as a society have crowned these kings. We have given them the authority to move and do as they wish. Their power has persuaded even the strongest of the strong because his royal courts are filled with nobles enjoying the so-called good life. The weak-minded would rather serve than become heirs to take the throne. Peasants have flocked to the crumbs that the king seldom throws at their feet, rather than maneuvering their way to one day feast at the court themselves. This king flexes his power through the mercy of those who desire to be what they are not capable of becoming. This is not the true meaning of a king.

Women are drawn by the power a king displays through his name being chanted in the crowds, and they eagerly throw themselves at any token he tosses their way. Women love him and men want to be him.

Is this what we have allowed society to shape the image of a king today? A twisted and ungrounded perception based on the media interpretation? In fact it is. Many young men will only know of this type of king; more than half will never know the true meaning of a real king. Our perception is based on what has been presented. We have let social network, jobs, magazines, music, and other influences create a false meaning of what a king really is. How do we change the perspective that has been anchored in the mind of men around the globe? No matter our race and ethnicity, we are all affected by this false representation of what a king is.

Until a real king presents himself, the view that has been displayed will continue to leave a false image of a king.

Potential is untapped success that can be possessed by anyone. It is distributed equally but is rarely utilized. Our male youth have the ability to choose their own fate by the decisions that they make. They have been given the power to rule themselves and those around them. Being a true king requires work and strategy; a basic principle lost amongst our youth. Just as in the game of chess, the king already possesses all the right pieces, but he must fully understand the capability of each piece to win. Without this, he will never be able to conquer the opposing side, and will be checked. There are no limits; the barriers have been broken, and the boundaries only exist within their own minds. They do not aspire to succeed and rule their true throne—that of honor and principles.

Potential is untapped success that can be possessed by anyone. It is distributed equally but is rarely utilized.

YOLO (You Only Live Once) has become a mentality created by false kings in which our youth have adopted and made it their way of life. This mentality has produced many servants and very few KINGS!!!

Chapter 5
Queen Who?

Just as the king, a queen also has her own position. In the game of chess, the queen is the most powerful piece. Although she can only move in a square that is not occupied, she is still solely responsible for the protection of the king.

Americans have drastically changed when it comes to their depiction of a queen. Throughout the entertainment industry, too many self-declared queens have ascended to a false throne simply through popularity and record sales. She talks openly about sex and even parades around half-naked. Is this a true queen? None of these so called queens can compare to Queen Elizabeth, a true monarch.

Although I would agree that beauty plays a part in a queen's image, why has that become the primary value of her throne? Beauty is much deeper than a commercially made up face or cosmetic surgeries. Beauty arises from within the soul and radiates out.

A true queen's value is not measured through her monetary possessions; rather, it is by the success of her kingdom. How much is she loved by those she rules? Chess gives the queen the ability to overpower her opponent, but her mobility is limited to vacancy. I interpret this as creating greatness from where there is nothing. By starting with nothing, she can create her own identity through her experiences, dreams, and ambitions.

Media shows our young ladies that in order to become a queen, they have to be a "Bad Bitch." Unfortunately, this has become their truth. They do whatever it takes by any means necessary to get attention. It does not matter who is affected by it. We emulate queens through photoshopped images, and dolled-up pictures. They categorize women by shapes and sizes, increasing the need to become thinner at any cost. This is what we as a society have come to recognize as beauty and strength—our role models. What happened to being modest, respectful, and ladylike? This is how we should define the true meaning of queen.

The media has reshaped our image of what a queen is.

The media has reshaped our image of what a queen is. Instead of using ideal role models such as the First Lady, they are provided with programs such as *Teen Mom, Sixteen and Pregnant*, and other reality TV shows that are rotting our youth's image. Reality shouldn't be getting pregnant at 16 and landing a starring role on TV. The facts are, when our lost queens are having babies as babies, they have a long hard road ahead of them. Unfortunately, their children tend to repeat the same cycle. Babies born to babies often come into unwed homes and many will end up being raised by a single parent or the state.

Somewhere along the way we have allowed our teens to adopt the habits of these reality images of scantily dressed pop stars and rappers. Teen girls idolize these images, that are anything but queen-like. They are dressing provocatively, and saying vulgarities on social media, while posting half-dressed pictures for all to see. Posts, status updates and tweets have become more important than their education. Keeping up with test scores and college applications have become dismissed. These same girls will lie in the arms of any guy to get attention, and sooner or later will find themselves on the outside looking in.

Are we really going to continue to allow our young women to believe that this is a queen's mentality? Have we accepted this as the meaning of a queen?

Every girl who is born is meant to be a queen. The mere fact that they are living and breathing gives them that privilege. They were born unadulterated to society's images and it is up to us to embody the proper teachings so they can reach their ultimate goal. Our queens possess the power to control and govern their life accordingly. The truth of the matter is that most of them are unaware that they are a queen. Sadly, some will become a servant to something or someone without ever knowing they could have been so much more.

Chapter 6
The Self-Destructing Queen

SHE WILL

Long hair and she don't care, willing to get down when and everywhere.

She will!

Looking like bag of money and smelling like a sack of onions but the hook of the song drives her wild, yep you guessed it, she will.

She wasn't interested in sports, let alone the debate team; all of her energy was towards making the Twerk team.

Daddy left a long time ago you see, so ever since then, she has been willing to find love wherever with whomever.

She Will is her theme song, because she's quick to prove a brotha wrong, let her tell it. She is About That Life.

She is always up for a challenge, quick to tell a chic "I betcha can't do it like me" like the song says.

Everybody knew her from the video she posted; got a thousand hits from her popping it in the club.

She celebrates with bottles of grey goose, it's normal for her to blame it on the alcohol.

Being about that life has gotten her bed sores from bed hopping and left empty because dudes only fill her up with their seeds only to leave her high and dry.

Her mom is willing to get down and bands will make her dance. Mama's says she gotta have a life too, the apple fell right by this tree.

A repeated cycle has become a re-run in this family.

Mama will, daughter will, even though auntie won't, but her cousins will.

Built like stallion, think like a snail, not the brightest crayon in the box; but if someone calls her a bad chic she is going to pop it for the night.

Daddy never took the time to date her, now she's dating other daddy's to keep the lights on.

She will do whatever you want even if it's with 2 or 3; she just wanna TurnUP.

Thrown from a car after the show, just as a seven day cleanse will run through you, the crew did her the same , now she has 8 different personalities living inside of her.

Oh she will get back out there to prove her friends what she's about, and how they can't hold her back.

Pregnant by a rapper named J-Money; she became a groupie ever since his performance at the local club.

Her baby needs Similac, that's cool because all J-Money wants is a big booty for his birthday.

Finally a taste of success; her baby daddy got his record deal. But he still records his tracks and sells dope out of the same house.

Yeah he raps about her, but as long as his bitches love him. He gone ball until fall, so she fights the chic around the corner because he knocked her up.

She's headed down to the welfare office, because she knows the government will definitely care for her child.

Selling a little weed is her side hustle, but if there is a trick to turn; She will.

Her body is the local waste ground.

Her pride is J-Money and his debut album.

She now feels Beyonce is a sellout, Oprah is extinct, and Michelle Obama is irrelevant to her, but now Diamond from the strip club is her role model.

She will degrade herself to no end, just to get all those likes on her Facebook post.

She takes pictures with her favorite rappers, oh yeah she is going to tag all of her haters.

She will post "'niggaz' ain't worth a damn."

She will tell you she goes to church and loves the Lord, but at the same time says God don't care; if he did why she broke?

She will smoke till she's higher than a kite.

She will tell you her baby is smart because he can sing the latest song from the radio yet he can't say his ABC's at 5 years old or count to 10.

She will say she's got this and she don't need a man; and you better stay out of her business and let her live her life.

Quiet as it is kept, life has lived her. She will do it all and then some, but, I bet she is not willing to tell you she is HIV positive.

She will...

She will die never knowing that she was meant to be a queen.

- Jay Barnett

A piece influenced by the song *She Will*

Something Has To CHANGE!

The next time you find yourself on the internet, visit places like Facebook, Instagram, or any of the other social media sites our teen and pre-teen girls hang out. Look at 10 open profiles and their content.

You will read and see what I see and hear on a daily basis in the schools—little girls talking about who they're going to hook up with; little girls talking about who's cheating on whom, who is fat, ugly, or a whore. Girls talking about how they Turnup the night before. Posting questions asking who smokes trees and talking about their baby daddy, and so forth.

Do you personally know any of these girls? Are they your kid? Can you see your kids' profiles? And if one or more was your child's, I ask of you, why? Why is your child displaying themselves in this manner? And if your answer is because you give your child freedom of speech or self-expression I say to you—THAT IS A COP OUT! That is NOT parenting—you are merely housing your child until they are old enough for you to kick them out your door. If she is not your child I ask you—how many of those profiles are profiles of your friend's kid, neighbor's kid, or acquaintance? Probably more than one. This is a major issue that is ruining our queens—our nation is losing its youth in our own backyards. It is NOT someone else's problem. It is everyone's problem! Our youth are on a self-destructive path due to our negligence.

There is a new definition of what a queen is today. She is the one who every man drools over, empties their bank account for, but still feels alone at the end of the day. What has happened to the true meaning of a queen? Superficial beauty has taken over our image of what a queen really is.

It isn't all about beauty, perfect figures and flawless faces. That is more often bought than born with. It's not about the clothes she's draped in, the "A" list parties, or where the cash flow emerges. It is the genuine queen-like mentality that is missing—those who aspire to be more than just arm candy.

Our queens have fallen into a trap of letting media develop their worth and define their beauty. According to a report by 2010 U.S. Department of Health and Human Services, young Americans ages 12 to 17 are actively consuming alcohol. If this is affecting more than half our youth, this is an issue we can't ignore. Amongst these stats, our young women ages 16 to 17 are the leading players. Today, the average age that an American girl has her first drink is 13; for a boy, it's 11.

One of the most common reasons teenage girls drink alcohol excessively is to escape problems or to cope with frustration or anger. Girls are more likely to drink because of family problems as opposed to peer pressure. When there is a lack of parenting or role models, the risk of pregnancy and sexually transmitted diseases increases dramatically. With the average age of our young girls' menstrual cycles starting at 12.5, there is no leeway for risky behavior.

What has happened to our youth? Where are the mothers—our queens? The fathers—our kings? Everyone is dodging the answers to these questions, or just turning their heads to the issues that have risen amongst our youth. Ignorance will not correct this ugly trend. It is time we take a serious look at ourselves. We have a serious problem that needs a solution and fast.

STD's and HIV are rapidly spreading throughout our younger generation. With our female youth having record low self-esteem issues, this is not a good combination. With our young females looking for acceptance where ever they can find it, this is downright frightening!

Various forms of media have developed our young ladies' ideal of what a woman should be. It dictates to them what is acceptable to deal with, when in fact, there are no real clear-cut boundaries anymore. According to reality TV shows, being pregnant at 16 is a quick ticket to fame, by throwing themselves at professional athletes or just to get their picture taking with a celebrity. Having multiple relationships before the age of 18 has become the norm— even when sex is involved. It is easy to continue on with the various ways media is forming inappropriate images of what we feel true reality should be to our youth, but unfortunately the media will never change. They are all about the money—money—money! It is we who must change them. It begins with us— and the manner in which we deal with our youth.

We are in a state of emergency. These are our little queens who are developing these behaviors based on false leaders. These same little self-destructive queens will have children and pass down those same behaviors. Our queens are self-destructing because we are letting them! This may be hard to comprehend but ownership has to start somewhere and it begins with us—men and women alike!

If we don't show these self-destructing queens exactly how valuable they are, how will they ever know?

We need true kings and queens who will step up and take these lost queens under their arms and guide them and set the example of what true kings and queens are. If we don't show these self-destructing queens exactly how valuable they are, how will they ever know? The media will never teach them the truth. It is our job as men, women, parents, teachers, and mentors, to help prepare them to rule.

Why is it that becoming a stripper has become the only "out" left available to our queens? Part of the reason is because the media announces those few that made it to "stardom" after starting a career as a stripper. What they don't show is the other 99% that didn't get so lucky and are living far less desirable lives. A survey taken by a guidance counselor at a Texas school where I spoke, presented a question. What was more appealing as a career? There options were attorney, doctor, teacher, or dancer. Almost half the young queens thought that being a dancer was more appealing. Why? Again, because music and television have presented them with a false illusion of fame and shows that men fawn over women who dance—and the less clothes, the better. What these young girls don't realize is that these same men doing all the drooling are not willing to take a stripper home to their mother or lift them to their rightful queen status; nor do they have a king mentality. It is purely animalistic lust.

Thank God for Michelle Obama for being such an influential role model. I was beginning to worry when Lady GaGa had more of an influence than Oprah. Nothing against Lady GaGa, she is successful at what she does, but that lifestyle or role is not for every young girl. I can't blame the media because they are driven by the mighty dollar. Society has created their market niche—sex sells! Nowadays men are finding women more desirable at an even younger age. Therefore men don't search beneath the surface, when the ads only advertise the container and not what is inside. Needless to say, these men neglect to realize that what is being presented to them is being done through a filtered lens.

Most stars are accompanied by an entourage of young scantily clad dancers. Our female stars are wearing less and less and expressing sexual innuendos in their lyrics and their dance. Sex has even carried over into our youth's cartoons. It appears there is nothing sacred anymore.

Unfortunately, a lot of these issues our young girls face relate back to daddy issues. Some have no knowledge of their father or any active positive male influence at all. The fault does not entirely lie with mothers. It takes two to tango and if the father of the young queen is nothing more than a sperm donor, that also plays a huge factor! Meanwhile, some get tangled in the parent's dating cycles. Some women are constantly looking for a partner but repeatedly pick the wrong ones, all while exposing their children to these fiascoes.

This leaves a lot of our youth, boys and girls alike, to rear themselves without proper guidance. This shouldn't be happening. One can try to pretend it is not their responsibility—but rather the parent's—but that would only be partially correct. But if no one steps up to the plate, who suffers? Not only will the children suffer, but society suffers overall in the long run. It takes a village to raise a child, but recently it seems that even the villages are dissipating due to a lack of participation.

Let's stop turning our heads away from young queens who are being left to their own devices. The negative behaviors that they are displaying are the results of being allowed to fly solo. Those same behaviors are the ones that will lead them to a future full of regrets. To be perfectly honest, a man will only respect a woman who respects herself. These young girls growing up without proper guidance will lack the self-respect they so rightfully deserve and should have.

Made Up-But Made Down

In marketing, what you have on display is what the shopper will consider buying. If you present less than a lady, you will be treated as such. Real queens walk like a queen, talk like a queen, most of all she will be treated like a queen because she understands who she is beyond her body.

I am a huge fan of makeup; I love what it can do for the people who need it to cover scars or other imperfections that bother them. I spoke on a topic a while back called "Covered Girl Uncovered" which dealt with the different elements of a cover girl from a predominently male perspective. My key point was that make-up should be used to enhance, not create an image that is false. Before applying the powder or bronzer you have to know who it is that you see in your mirror. The mirror only reflects the external, while your character reflects the internal. What you see is who you are. It is so important to define yourself beyond the foundation, mascara and lip gloss that everyone is falling in love with. So many of our young queens are misled through commercials, weight loss products, and magazine covers because they are unaware of reality—what is actually behind those airbrushed images. It does not matter what you paint your face with; if a queen does not know her real self, she will always be insecure without it. Make up does not cover up the inside; it may hide the dark spots and blemishes but it can't hide the internal wounds. I challenge the female readers to pull a young queen to the side and teach her that beauty is within and that it is not external.

Female readers: pull a young queen to the side and teach her that beauty is within and that it is not external.

There are so many young queens who are physically well, but on the inside they are just broken little girls. They have bought into the lies that if they put a little war paint on, it will make them feel better, but it doesn't fix the insecurities. Adult queens need to help the aspiring queens to deal with the hurts and pains that others prey on and use against them. Adult kings are needed to teach our young girls that they are beautiful without the makeup. We all need to help them understand that they are precious beyond rubies. So many young queens today lack positive male figures in their lives. Any woman who didn't receive attention from her dad, in most cases, seeks affirmation from a man. If they are not careful they will come across men who prey on their minds, because they can see it a mile away. That is why it's so important to teach queens to wait for dressing up as a woman and wearing makeup until they are mentally mature enough to distinguish between a genuine king approach or a man on the hunt. There are plenty of years for made up faces, but only so many developmental years to raise a queen. There is one thing that will always ring true—the real woman is just a shade away from the brush.

Queens Are Not for Sale!

Other types of self-destructive behavior some of our queens display is the belief that everything has a price. All-star weekend and other major sporting events have become an auction of sorts for females of various ages looking to score with a millionaire. Females who have a Wal-Mart budget with a Nordstrom outfit are looking and willing, by any means necessary, to be chosen by the hottest, fastest, wealthiest athletes or whoever is willing buy their innocence. This has become reality and just another part of life for some. The sad thing about this is that our young queens who see this behavior begin to believe that selling your body and soul is a quick and easy way to become successful. A true queen is not for sale. Her value is not represented by tangible items; it is through her integrity and self-worth.

Queen Elizabeth will not argue with anyone or try to explain who she is because she knows. There is a huge difference between guessing and knowing. You must know that you cannot be bought at any price. No bag, car, house, or any material possession should wow you to the point that you are willing lay to down your integrity.

To our queens; you are priceless! You are blessed to replenish the earth for your king, not to be a jump off for some loser and his crew. Your smile was meant to bless the lives you will touch, not to be of service to a guy who is only looking to check you off his list. Your beauty is yours to keep and yours to give, not to be a wall post on everybody's cell phone. Queens—you are to rule your territory until the right king proves he can rule with you and not rule over you. Know that you are priceless and you deserve the best because you are a queen.

Chapter 7
Tools Needed To Find
The Lost Kings And Queens

A plumber without his tools is a plumber that is not going to get the job done. How can a handy man be handy if he never has any tools with him? Tools are instruments, devices, or anything that can aid one in getting the job done. They are either mental or physical and are important to accomplish any task. When it comes to finding our lost kings and queens, if you don't have the right tools, you can't be effective in your quest.

The only way anyone can be ready for the task of recapturing our lost youth is to possess the necessary tools. There is nothing written in stone as to what tool(s) will be needed at any given time, so your toolbox will need to be large and very refined. Every situation is different. A carpenter doesn't just use a hammer in his craft. Some projects require him to use the entire toolbox, where others may only require a screwdriver. You have to be equipped with the right instruments. Our lost youth are faced with different challenges that require patience, love, time, a listening ear, and even the ability to capture the unsaid. Whatever it is, you have to be prepared and stay alert.

The following are 5 of the most important tools you will need to find our lost and the needed elements it takes to reach them.

Be Reliable—the number one thing I hear youth say is they are sick of people coming in and out of their life. No matter what role you play, you need to be reliable and not just when it is convenient for you. Be a man or woman of your word. Do what you say you are going to do and be where you are supposed to be. Don't get sidetracked by things that are not important and things that do not contribute to the success of our youth. This generation is able to read insincerity a mile away. If you are not going to be reliable don't start the process of searching for the lost. Far too many young people have little or no role model which in turn leads them to seek out their own. Most are not properly equipped to distinguish between positive and negative attention, and too many times they fall prey to those with ill intent. We have to stop this and save our kings and queens!

Be Determined—Anytime you are working with our lost youth, be prepared for a challenge. They are not easily won over, due to the series of let downs in their lives. They have built walls so that further disappointments don't hurt as much. They portray that they know it all as a defense mechanism. You have to go in knowing that if you're not immediately embraced, it is not about you, it is about them and their sense of reservation. Determination + Resilience= Results! If there is no determination the option to quit will always be exercised. Emanate positive determination!

Be Positive—Our youth deal with enough negativity in their surroundings, whether it be school, home, or just constant peer pressure. Provide uplifting words, leave the pessimistic attitude at home, or don't talk to them at all. I tell our youth all the time that life can be what you want it to be. The glass does not have to be half empty; it can be full all the time. This is a way of thinking, so if we can change their thinking we can change their paths. Positive words give life to a dying situation and with the choice of our words we can develop these lost kings and queens to be positive.

Be Diligent—Most people who lack success, do so because they lack the diligence to finish. It takes tenacity and willpower to stay with it. Even when you second guess yourself, you must persevere. Diligence is essential when working with our lost! Society has already thrown the towel in on our lost youth before giving them a fair chance. Sadly, many parents have given up on their own blood. It is imperative that we take responsibility, and in the process we will ultimately change the direction of our youth for the better. However, our mindset must be set on the finish line before we start. Stay the course and they will come around. Our youth just want to know that we will not give up on them.

Prayer is a necessity...Fighting on your knees with folded hands is the best defense any of us can use in the time of battle.

Be Prayerful—Last, but most definitely not least of all these tools, being kings and queens of prayer is a necessity. Contrary to popular opinion, fighting on your knees with folded hands is the best defense any of us can use at the time of battle. Prayer can mend the mind of any lost king.

We must realize that there is always room for improvement and acknowledge that getting help is a great thing. I was so unskilled in so many areas of my life to the point that I was disgusted with my own inadequacy. Being unlearned or undeveloped doesn't necessarily have to be a bad thing, as long as you do not allow yourself to become stagnant in life. You always have the opportunity to do better no matter your age. My hope is that regardless of what stage you are in your personal life, you will always see greatness within yourself and strive to maximize your full potential. In return, help our youth strive to reach their full potential as well. Let us come together and raise our lost kings and queens. Develop them to meet their God-given purpose, which is to rule their thrones with greatness. Our youth must find their way back to royalty.

Chapter 8
Communicate To Navigate

Communication has changed so much within the past few years. Information is conveyed through a mass of tech devices and far less than the actual face to face and voice to voice from days gone by. Times have changed tremendously since Alexander Graham Bell's invention of the telephone. The massive new ways we communicate now can get overwhelming and so much is lost. People of all ages are glued to their cell phones, computers, iPads, etc. When I was a kid I talked to my friends and sisters with a Walkie-Talkie; being able to talk to someone without seeing them was so cool to me. This has all been replaced with things like FaceTime, Skype, and the most popular of them all, texting.

Our world moves at a much faster pace than it ever has. People are constantly on the go. Jobs are more demanding and everybody is in the rat race of getting more. Chasing this high paced life, things have been run over and left behind. One of the most important things that we have left is communication: person to person, boss to employees, and even parent to child.

In most cases, we rarely make time to connect with people face to face in fear of missing something in the few minutes that it may take. We covet quick information and answers; we don't have time for research or investigation. Libraries are becoming abandoned buildings. Due to all the devices that are presented, we are distancing ourselves from physical contact and more importantly developing human connection—we are furthering the distance between one another. We are losing the foundation to build intimate relationships with people in general. Some people would rather text than talk in person. This affects our lost kings and queens. The most important thing in growth and nurturing is bonding.

The bonds that our youth once had with their parents and even neighbors have been replaced with communication tools that lack any real sense of emotion.

In some of my interaction with parents and teachers I've heard them say teens do not listen or respect them. My response is, "How do you communicate with them?" The key to communication is presentation; if one cannot communicate how can they navigate a conversation? The biggest problem I see is that many parents and school officials are out of touch with this generation. Being able to relate to the person you are communicating with is very important. In order to bridge the gap of communication we must understand where an individual is coming from. Communication is a key factor in how we will find a lost king or queen, but it will be a challenge. When we relate, then we can communicate, and everyone will walk away with an understanding. This method will be effective when communicating with our youth.

Change Your Approach

Too many time adults approach teens the wrong way because of how someone related to them. Think of how often we have found ourselves repeating the same or similar phrases that our parents said to us as children. More than likely, many of them are outdated with time. The value may still be golden, but the delivery may need some tweaking.

Understanding the personal makeup of the person you are talking to will help in effectively communicating with them. No two children are alike. Every situation is charged with a different approach; it first starts with respect. Respect is earned, not given. Just because we may hold a place of authority or we're the adult in the situation does not give us automatic respect. Teens will respect those who respect them. I can't blame them sometimes either. Too many times they are disrespected, so in return they build a wall that may come across as disrespect. This might just be their shield of protection. It is easier to distract the "enemy" in their mind by acting out, raising their voice, using derogatory language and other negative mannerisms when speaking with an adult. It keeps the adult from finding out what is really going on in their minds, what real problems and hurts they are experiencing. I guarantee that if we change our approach, our message will be heard. It may not happen overnight, especially in the most troubled youth, but it will happen. But they first have to feel safe in order to let us in. This takes time and consistency.

Society has already cursed the youth into a pattern of self-destruction, selfishness, and grasping for immediate gratification, while leaving them full of uncontrollable emotions. Knowing this, there is no reason to reinvent the wheel; we simply have to change the direction in which it turns. But we as adults have a tendency to over think things, complicating them more than they need to be. They are teenagers—they have historically been perceived as "know it alls," so when we preach to them that they don't know it all, our words are falling on deaf ears. It is us who need to change our approach.

If we are to find the lost, we must communicate in a way that is not judgmental or controlling. This is "Generation I": the iPhone; iPad; iPods; iTouch; "I want it my way"; and the most popular of them all "I will shut down on you." The reason our approach is so important is that we cannot allow our lost kings and queens to shut down and go into isolation. We must understand this is not the old days where we could say whatever we wanted and the youth would respond. This generation will simply shut us out if we come at them the wrong way. So we win by humbling ourselves to understand where they are. These kings and queens are faced with adult issues and problems. Times have changed, so we must change if we are going to be successful in communicating with our lost.

Texting vs. Talking

It seems as if everyone has an electronic device glued to their hand; isolated from the human touch, eye contact or talking. People still connect, but at the touch of a send button. Our voices have become delivered by a finger rather than through audible inflections. Reading body language is a lost art and completely unknown to our youth. Body language was considered to be a priceless tool of communication, but not in this new age. Texting defeated this by a landslide; saying whatever one wants without actually speaking real words. There are no emotions or feelings; these have been replaced by emoticons.

We can't be serious. This way of life is disconnecting us from our teens. Texting our feelings is not effective communication. Typing "Hey, I text you," may be a sufficient attempt, but it is not effective. Many parents communicate with their kids through texting now than ever, because they feel texting is easier than talking. Nothing will ever take the place of a face-to-face conversation between two people or in an open setting within a group.

Parents wake up and drink the coffee. Don't just smell it, take a sip and savor the taste. The disconnection between our teens is our failure to connect no matter the cost. This is unfortunate. Yes, we have to work more hours to make a decent living and life itself has become more demanding. Meanwhile, we could be saving so much money by stopping the unlimited text packages on our cell phones! Not only will we save money, but we might just save our youth from becoming statistics!

It takes effort to speak verbally even though in some situations it can be a challenge. However this is a challenge we should embrace—not avoid! Our teens are losing out on basic social skills because we have made it acceptable to constantly text rather than talk. No matter how we look at it, it's not a great method of communication. It is an electronic telegraph that doesn't take any physical interaction at all. More than 70 percent of Americans are texting. This creates a problem for our youth to communicate in the future. Texting has become a predecessor for a new form of communication that does not require physical contact. This makes it easier for everyone to be even more isolated. It is a dangerous trend that we have adopted in our society to communicate with others.

Knowing how to articulate our feelings has become obsolete. I have nothing against modern technology, as long as it is not used to replace human interaction the way God had intended it to be—up close and personal.

If we are going to raise our youth to reach their full potential, it will mean putting down the phone and actually starting conversations face-to-face. Effort is made, not given. It's our responsibility to bridge the gap of communication and create situations for open dialogue.

Social media has given our lost kings and queens a platform for communication because the home front is failing in its duties. Yet we are easily surprised when our youth do the unexpected. Who's at fault? We all have to take some of that responsibility.

Power In Words

As an inspirational speaker, I am cautious of the words that come out of my mouth. Before uttering a word, I filter every word through my thought process. I ask myself, "If I say this, will it live in the hearts of the youth forever?" Words can shape or steer the direction of one's life, including my

If you don't want to hear it again, don't say it. Our youth are sponges and will soak in everything they hear, even when we doubt we have their attention.

own. Just as I know how powerful they can be, the long lasting effect they can have can be good or bad. It is important for parents, mentors, educators and leaders to be just as thoughtful with their words as with their delivery. Your words will take root for the better or worse. Our youth are sponges and soak in everything they hear, even when we doubt we have their attention. My grandmother would always say, "If you don't want to hear it again don't say it."

I interpret this as "we do as we see and say what we hear." If we don't want our children repeating the negativity, let us not speak or act negatively. Our youth emulate everything they see and hear.

Interestingly enough, many adults still feel they can say whatever they want since they are older, no matter the age of their audience. Age does not equate to maturity. For example, I have childhood friends who are products of the words that were spoken to them as children. My buddy's mom would say all the time, "Your daddy wasn't nothing so you ain't gonna be nothing." Yet I couldn't understand the surprise when my friend was sent to jail. Why? I was baffled at first until I realized that we are a product of our environments. How can someone expect greatness to be birthed from negative impartation? It doesn't work that way; all of us are reflections of what we have seen and heard.

Music has such a strong influence because the words shape the imaginations of these lost kings and queens. The lyrics speak to them whether negative or positive; they hear money, cars, clothes, and dope, which, in their minds, represents success. In turn, this is what they aspire to become or pursue. The same works for us who are in a role to navigate the lost. We must be mindful of the words we speak, because words are like seeds in the ground. If you plant an apple seed and nurture it daily, apples will be the fruit that you harvest, not oranges. We cannot speak negatively and expect to have positive results. "Life and death is in the power of the tongue," as the bible states. I once heard a wise man say that the pink tornado is one of the most devastating forces of nature. He was referring to the human tongue.

If we want our youth to be receptive to our words, we must change our approach and create personal interaction with them; one that nurtures them to not only be the best that they can be, but the best they are meant to be. Our youth will rule their territory by the words that are spoken to them over time. Everything in life is a cycle; the cycle that is created will be a rotation of the next. It will only change if we change our method of communication. We need to speak words that uplift and encourage our youth to be great in whatever they choose.

We need to be more supportive of our youth and do it with positive reinforcement. The power in our words can change a negative path that is already set in motion into a positive one. We should all hope to inspire with our words, conversation, and interaction with the lost. A strong word can change a weak mind.

Chapter 9
Teach Process Not Success

Our youth are heavily exposed to TV, stylish headphones with the newest "I" gadget, and music roaring through their sensitive ear drums. Studies show that some will suffer from hearing loss by the time they reach middle age. Most teenagers can be spotted with an expensive device purchased by their parents who desperately want to give their children everything they lacked in their youth. It's likely this treatment has created a poor work ethic amongst our youth. No work is required of them, because everyone gets a trophy.

I asked a father of a student I work with why he felt he didn't need to deal with his daughter on a daily basis. He said because he gives her anything to keep her quiet and out of his way. I asked him if he was serious to which he replied, "I don't have time to get into conversations with my kids, so my money speaks for me."

I guess he checked me. The problem with this situation is that it is a reality nowadays for some parents. They give their kids toys, gadgets, electronics, games, and flatscreens to keep them occupied. Some of these parents use TV as a babysitter. However, this is not how parenting should be, not if you want to raise productive adults. Unfortunately, so many parents have replaced the time and attention their children deserve with monetary things, hoping to appease their need for affection. This is giving our youth the wrong perception, creates poor work ethics and does not teach our youth character and accountability. Shame on these parents. No one should just give you what you want to make you go away; there should be a no child left behind policy in the real world, not just in schools.

Due to the lack of outdoor participation, kids have become more confined to their rooms and have secluded themselves from activities that challenge their basic social skills. After all, this is Generation I: iPod's, iPhone, iTouch, I want this and I want that. But how can a child know what is reasonable for them? Isn't that the adult's responsibility to ensure that their child is well balanced? I don't understand that.

We have lost tons of kings and queens because when work is involved, they quit. Why? All society teaches is success, not the process it takes to achieve it. We teach that "possessions" equal success—cars, clothes, nice homes— and we forget that those possessions are only monetary. They do not equate to one's real feeling of success. Success comes from within. No one wakes up successful; real success is not money that was won or inherited. It is a process to understand that one must be willing to work beyond pay. When we teach the process, our kings and queens will understand that the things that require the most work and take the longest to obtain will last the longest.

The Butterfly Effect

When we are born we are in a protected sac called caul. This shields us from all the harmful things that can take place during a pregnancy. The caul is our cocoon. From a fetus to a baby, a cocoon to a beautiful butterfly; everything in life has a system; a process. When we omit the process we can't function in an environment that was geared for our habitat; then we die. The lost kings and queens don't understand that success is a process. There is no overnight fame. If there is one, it lasted overnight, and at what cost? We cannot avoid teaching the butterfly effect. The butterfly effect is the desire for a particular thing, where even the slightest change can result in two significantly different outcomes. The purpose of learning and being trained is so that one may be prepared for whatever is thrown in one's path.

Our youth are lost because everyone wants to be a winner before even training for the race. There is no process because everyone gets awarded for playing. Therefore we have premature, functionally illiterate individuals living among us that are missing the mark. They cannot socialize without having a device in hand. They can't build anything, and good luck getting them to identify with others. Our youth struggle to do basic math without a device—how can we expect them to manage their future? They fail to take responsibility for the simplest of things, such as missing the bus— blaming their parents for not waking them. What happens when they're late for their job? I will tell you—they won't have one and society will be paying their bills. They have no accountability because accountability takes too much effort for a parent to instill.

We have a serious problem because of television shows that flaunt celebrities' success. They only show the house, and not what it took to secure the house, nor the hard work and many hours given. This creates the perspective that it happened without a process. No one wants to struggle anymore; if something causes them blood, sweat, or tears, most will quit. The generation of "go-getters" is becoming obsolete and now we have birthed the "go get it for me" generation.

It may be cute when they are little, making a parent "feel" needed, but it won't be "cute" when this same child cannot get a job on their own. I don't solely blame social media, music, electronics, or TV; it is the parents, teachers, mentors, and pastors. We should hold ourselves more accountable.

We have taken a back seat to a lost generation that refuses process. Yet we have refused to take the time to teach them that this process even exists! The cocoon teaches the butterfly how to struggle and fight for its own survival. The only way our youth are going to know that they are ready for the world is if they have been taught what it means to fight for what they want, handle struggles, and learn the tenacity needed to go after their dreams. But as long as we continue to "get" everything for them, they will never need a reason to step up.

What Is Success?

We have this misconception of what success is because our world is built on the "haves" and the "have nots." That is just the reality of society. There will always be the poor and the rich. Everyone's definition of success will not be the same. Our lost youth are misguided due to the skewed thinking of a greedy nation. Everything is about "more this" and "more that" even when it is more than we can ever need. Nice cars and chains dripping in "iced out" diamonds does not equate to success. Perception is not everything, most of the time things are not what they appear to be.

I always say look beyond the surface. If we took a deeper look into what we call success, we would change our perception. Let's encourage the lost to know that success is whatever they want it to be. They are the kings and queens and they are in control of their success, not a car, house, clothes, or money itself. All of that is monetary, so it will never change the person, only the circumstances. It's important we teach this method because so many are selling their souls for a façade.

Money only enhances who you are. It is a magnifier to the real you. If you are self-esteem broke and you take measures to increase your self-esteem, money may change the outer you, but your low self-esteem will always be an issue. So is that success? No. If success meant wealth, why do we have so many

Money only enhances who you are; it is a magnifier to the real you.

financially affluent people unhappy with their lives. It is our job to teach our youth that money is merely a tool, not a fixer of core problems.

I heard one of the most powerful statements from Pastor Charles Perry III, a minister at my church: "Money is a great servant, but if you're not careful, it will be a horrible master." Success is within all of us, if we choose to seek it. Before you start measuring up your success by possessions and other worldly things, make sure you have secured success in your soul. Ask yourself—if I lost everything I had, would I still like myself? Would I be proud of myself? Could I hold my head up and know I had the skill set to start all over again? Would I be successful? Remember, we have set the bar for our youth, and if the lost kings and queens are found, and we lift them, then that is true SUCCESS.

Work + Dedication –Procrastination = SUCCESS

There are many formulas that equate to a positive outcome. This formula goes without saying; it's been tried, tested, and proven. This equation is a must have for life, relationships, business, and friendships. In everyone's efforts to find these lost kings and queens it is going to take time, work, and dedication to achieve success. I am committed to the purpose of this call and married to this cause for change. I hope you are too. Many of us never commit to anything and some appear to commit to quitting—sad but true.

We develop our attitude based on the task at hand. For example, when on a well-planned trip, we are excited. However, as soon as a road block is thrown in our path, our attitude changes. The smiles turn to frowns and our motivation gets dampened, if not halted like the road block. If we want our youth to be motivated to work and dedicate themselves, it starts with us—the mentors, parents, and teachers. We must be the gas in the engine and the atlas to their destination so they know what direction to take. If we are half committed, then they will be, too. If we want them to make it to their destination in life, we have to give them the tools and examples to help them navigate.

Procrastination is the death of so many dreams and it is kryptonite to a vision.

Procrastination is the death of so many dreams and it is the kryptonite to a vision; this is a lazy spirit. Most of our issues today are self-imposed because we as guardians, educators, and parents have failed in our responsibilities simply because we were too lazy to go the extra mile. Let's not just blow the trumpet, let's adhere to the sound and pick up our step. Everyone that has an influence in the life of a young king and queen, step your game UP! Come prepared to dedicate yourself and leave the "I will later" attitude behind. Imagine if our coaches, teachers, or our neighbor across the street had procrastinated about supporting us? Where would we be? Our youth needs us. Too many are lost and don't have a clue. All they know is what they want, but none of them know how to get what they want or how to even survive. Let us not procrastinate; our teens are waiting for our support.

Too Comfortable With Death

Have you ever been comfortable to the point where you trust the very thing that was once threatening? Try getting comfortable with something you once feared, like death. Sometimes life is so uncomfortable that you become secure in your thoughts, even if they are skewed. Life happens to all of us at some point; some of us become pessimistic, others cynical, and some have a glass half empty attitude.

I became too comfortable. Life had become hopeless and another sad song that I was tired of singing. The things mama told me as a kid became a foreign language because the world was so unfair. I constantly asked myself why? Why me? Why my family? Why did my dad leave us? Why had my world stopped revolving? Or so I thought.

A lot of questions were asked of God, but I was given no answers to fill in the blanks. God became another name that I spoke of less and less; my heart no longer cried out to Him. My heart bled with the blood of disappointment; of anger that He didn't fix my family. The more I prayed, the more I felt life disappearing like the dew in the morning on the front lawn.

My friends were few, so I isolated myself with four guys that introduced themselves as the Walls. The Walls became my confidants and comrades. They were great in my eyes because they spoke of things I had never heard. Their language became common to me, so I started to speak their language to the point that I was comfortable with them. They were great at keeping secrets; I could cry and they wouldn't tell.

I could have all types of thoughts and they wouldn't judge me. The Walls were always available when life would happen to me. Every day with open ears they would listen. They gave their undivided attention in the evenings because they knew our friendship wouldn't be interrupted. The more time I spent with them they began to notice my weakness and the areas in my life that knocked me back the hardest.

The Walls were my number one fans in the game I often spoke of called life. I felt as if I was losing time after time, so my fans suggested I speak with a friend of theirs, since most of my conversations were based on quitting the game of life. My fans reached out to their buddy Death. Little did I know, he was a friend of the Walls all along.

Death had sat in and listened to all of our conversations, everything I had spoken; he knew me inside and out. He told me I had become comfortable with him and I didn't even know it. I replied how so? He said, when you came into the Walls environment, you turned the lights off, and that meant you welcomed me to attend. Whenever you spoke of yourself being a failure and how you didn't want to live, I was listening. Remember when you spoke of quitting the game of life? So I thought I would formally introduce myself.

I had become comfortable with someone I used to fear. I had become vulnerable to my emotions, thoughts, and to the voice of the enemy. I had opened the door for someone who didn't knock; I opened the door without looking out the peep hole. I had become stuck between my feelings that so often before had led me to open my mouth and question; yet I stopped asking.

See, I became vulnerable to the Walls family, only to find out that they were in on the plot the whole time. Too close for comfort was a saying that I heard in passing. At that moment

I was beyond that point of passing. Because death had become comfortable with my story, he felt he could offer the solution.

My lack of judgment had me debating with someone who knew my every move and thought, because I had fallen victim to his false sense of security.

Death was dating suicide and invited me to be a part of their relationship.

For most of us, curiosity will kill us. But I was saved by a friend who saw the whole setup. This friend waited for his moment to intervene.

I became comfortable with suicide and I almost took my life. I have learned that comfort is a place that only the weak minded reside. If you get too close you will receive comfort from the wrong thing.

Thanks to my great friend for listening in on the Walls.

Jesus was the friend that stayed closer than any other could have.

It was his interference that saved my life.

Chapter 10
Untimely Death

We are losing our children at an alarming rate, simply because they haven't been taught the proper life skills necessary to deal with problems that occur in their lives. This leads them to deal with their problems in a self-destructive manner. Sometimes this results in drug use, harming themselves or tragically, suicide. It's an unbelievably alarming statistic, but each year there are approximately 10 youth suicides for every 100,000 suicides committed by adults.

Statistics have also shown that every 2 hours and 11 minutes a person under the age of 25 commits suicide. These numbers indicate that suicide is the 3rd leading cause of death among teens and young adults. In an article written by senior medical writer Daniel J. Denoon, he states that the suicide rate has drastically increased to 76% with girls between the ages of 10-14 and 32% in girls 15-19 years of age. The number for young boys has risen 9% in those who are between the ages of 15-19. These numbers prove that we are in a fight to save the lives of our youth.

The pressure that our youth experience each day, whether it is from peers, parents or other authority figures, can be powerful in two ways; either it will create a diamond that will sparkle like the sun or it may cause their lights to dim. The amount of pressure placed on teens in this day and age is pushing them to their breaking point and is impacting families all across the country. I can remember a time when suicide was primarily associated with Native Americans or caucasians. This problem is no longer experienced by a particular race. Suicide is a global issue with no respect for race, gender, or socioeconomic status.

How do we stop it? Until we can place a deeper value on life, it will never fully be appreciated in the way that God intended. As a speaker and mentor, I place emphasis on how precious life is. I often share my own testimony about sitting on the floor in front of my bed getting ready to take my own life.

I will never forget feeling like a failure because my football career had failed. I felt that I didn't have anything to live for at that point. At that time in my life, I honestly believed that to be true. It wasn't until I heard God's voice that I made a choice to live.

There are a lot of lost kings and queens who have chosen not to live. They have fallen victim to the voice that tells them death is the easy way out. What is so sad is that the graveyard is one of the richest places on earth. It is full of unfulfilled dreams, aspirations, and great people who will never be able to fulfill their purpose. My heart goes out to the youth who have tragically lost their lives to suicide. We will never know what could have become of them had they been found in time.

Let's take responsibility for our lost youth and compel them to reach out and show them there is always hope. We must attempt to shed light on some of the things that are pushing our children into these situations. Teens are relentlessly being bullied, struggling with their sexuality, and confused about which clique or gang to join. Some are struggling to find their identity while others are pressured to change their identity. It is up to us as leaders and facilitators to stop these untimely deaths. Our job is not to judge, but rather to shower them with love and acceptance, for whomever they choose to become.

The Power In Isolation

One day I found myself sitting in a closed room, isolated from the world, angry at my father because he divorced my mother. I was bitter about my life and resented my past because it haunted my future. Darkness set over my eyes as I thought about all the evil things I could do to the people who had hurt my family. I didn't have a care in the world because I believed that the world was against me. All of these thoughts and feelings took place while I was alone in my room with my "new group of friends."

Self-isolation is not a good place to be, but it is caused by experiencing rejection from the one thing or person who you long for their attention. Many kings and queens have come to resent their father or mother because they were not a part of their lives while they were growing up. Some have also developed "daddy issues" because of the lack of a male influence. These lost youth spend so much of their lives trying to figure out the whys, until they reach the point where it becomes too much for them and they eventually break.

Isolated teens tend to drift amongst crowds, struggling to find their way. Most are not very social and tend to distance themselves because they believe they have been thrown away. As human beings we all have the need to feel wanted, whether it is from family, friends, or society. We all want to be accepted for who we are, but the world isn't perfect and doesn't always operate in that manner. People will always find something to ridicule and will harass the weak.

In many cases the teens who have committed suicide began by isolating themselves. The thing that you should know about isolation is that it's tricky, because there is usually only one person talking and that same person is answering. Rather than having someone provide valuable feedback to the individual, they tend to only see their side of the problem. Isolation allows the individual to focus on every negative thing about their personality and life. As they begin to only focus on the negative aspects of their lives, the walls that they have built around themselves will begin to engulf them.

Eventually what was only a thought can easily become an action.

As the walls begin to close in around the individual, eventually what was only a thought can easily become an action. I can tell you from my own experience, when you get comfortable with death and with the thought of what the next step involves, it tends to become much easier to follow through with the act. Our job is to reach out to any child who is isolating themselves from the crowd or from the circle. Too many times, we turn our heads and say it's not our problem. But it is our problem. If you have firsthand knowledge about a child who is spending too much time alone, it's your responsibility to become involved and ask questions.

Encouraging them to socialize and open up about what is going on can help them realize that they are not alone. By ignoring the situation and not becoming involved, that reclusive child may see the final act as their only solution.

We must become familiar with the signs of isolation, especially parents. Please pay attention to your children. Don't allow your children to go to their rooms instead of interacting with the family. This only allows them to create distance and begin isolating themselves from everyone who cares about them.

As a parent, become more active in your child's life. The more involved you are, the more they will feel comfortable to let you inside. Isolation is brought about by the individual's belief that there is no one who cares about who they are or what they do.

Parents and other authority figures must hold themselves accountable and ask children how they are and what they are feeling. It does not matter if it is our child or not. If adults don't isolate themselves, then teens will not isolate either.

Saying Nothing Equals Tragedy

There was a young lady that posted a weapon on her social media page and instead of her receiving comments about her wellbeing, she received a ton of likes. Yes, that is the world we live in. We praise foolishness, we celebrate ignorance, we bless buffoonery and when there is a serious matter we choose to ignore it. Tragically, this young lady took her own life with the weapon that was displayed. How many people ignored her cry for help? I'm sure the many friends on her social media site were silent as well. Now there is another young life tragically lost, because she wasn't found.

We have become a selfish society. We have conditioned ourselves to believe that if it's not our problem we are not required to act. This is the wrong mind set. Not saying anything to this young woman ended in a tragic loss for her family and friends. Imagine if someone would have had the courage to say something to her or her family. Many times we tend to talk about the wrong issues and avoid the issues that we need to be discussing.

Being silent is the wrong way to respond to these issues. That's the thing about social media. It's a platform, but not a voice. People are able to sit and type whatever they like, but it will never take the place of someone speaking to an individual directly. Speaking life into a deadly situation, is what we should strive to do in our daily lives in order to find these kings and queens. The lost are taking their own lives because this has become an easy solution for some. They make a permanent decision for a temporary situation. In some areas a single act of suicide has resulted in a series of suicides taking place in the same school.

What has happened to our society that we have taken the joy out of the lives of our children, and that they only see suicide as their only option?

All of the material things that we give them are not enough to substitute becoming actively involved in their lives. What they need, instead of the latest pair of shoes or jeans is someone to show them that they truly matter and what they have to say is important. Our children are growing up in a world full of opportunities for success, but also for failure. Instead of turning their minds away from the worst, it only seems to push them further over the edge. The world has no love; it can't love anyone—it doesn't have a heart. So when these lost teens run to this cold world, it only offers them a short term fix. Their options are drugs, sex, and alcohol. But none of these are the answers they need. How many times have we heard the news of a teen suicide, and said the same thing, I didn't know it was that bad. My question for these people is, did you ever ask? If we choose not to ask, all we are left with is the need to attend a funeral that didn't need to take place. We need to start becoming assertive in our children's lives in order to stop these senseless acts and save our lost youth.

Preserve The Lost

We have become so distracted by focusing on our own lives that we have forgotten our main focus, our children. Each day I hear adults say that teens will continue to do what they want and not listen to them, so why bother? There is so much power in the future. We tend to focus on the here and now, and we forget that our teens are the future. Being ambitious is great; we all should aspire to be better at what we do. To preserve something means to keep it. God has entrusted us with the ability to be an example to our children. By preserving our lost teens we give them life, opportunity, and something to live for.

Death is something that we all have to face in our lives. However, that is a choice that God should make for us. We cannot be our brother's keepers by standing and watching our teens fall victim to the perils and circumstances they face. Preservation is a must. The longer our teens are here with us, they

By preserving our lost teens we give them life, opportunity, and something to live for.

will get better at handling problems as they arise. Our youth will never know how great they can be in ruling their kingdom if they die young. I challenge everyone to take time out of their day and speak to someone who may be in a dark place. Let the lost kings and queens know that they are valuable and that this world needs them. The world will be a better place if we stop judging and start preserving.

Chapter 11
Criticism And Discipline

Opinions are like choices, everybody has one. Too often, people like to give their two-cents and criticism without any relevant information. Not always is this done with good intentions. We usually would not care to hear other's opinions, especially if we feel their opinion is not conducive to the situation. Many times criticism can be negative if it is not coming from a solid place. The issue people have is being criticized for how they feel or think according to their own experiences. If we are not careful, our critiques will bleed into how we discipline. This will surely affect how we parent.

No matter how one states it, we're all reflections of our past experiences which have formed our criticism, whether it is positive or negative. We need to open our minds as parents, teachers, and guardians about how criticism affects our youth. I want to help people in general, understanding that discipline should not be used as a method of control or manipulation through authority. Discipline is a system of training that corrects for better judgment next time. But when one talks about criticism it's simple to me. It is an evaluated or analytical expression about an issue based upon someone else's opinion.

My questions to adults are:

- How do you criticize?
- Is the criticism coming from a solid place?
- Does positive reinforcement follow your criticism?
- Parents and/or guardians, how do you discipline? Are you disciplining your children out of anger? What is the correct disciplinary tool? There is a fine line between both of these two worlds, but they are similar in some ways.

Sadly enough, a lot of parents and adults have become cynical due to their experience with life or people in general. In some cases these two worlds mesh because of what might have happened to them. Some parents have become adamant in their way of thinking "I know what is best" and "this is how it is going to be." If you have failed in this area, it's okay. You can always correct, and try again. I will provide new strategies and a different way of how to discipline and critique effectively.

The old ways of discipline are in the past. The current generations of teens have changed in their behavior, and they no longer display respect for their elders. This is partly due to the onset of those who lack parenting skills and rest it in the hands of society. For the record, I support the old ways of discipline. However, when the controversy erupted from "lawmakers" that spanking your child was abuse and punishable by the law and the courts, our youth were empowered, but for the wrong reasons. It is often held over their heads as a threat to parents that have never raised a hand to their child. Some teens have taken advantage of the system. Unfortunately, some of these parents are forced to deal with the repercussions from courts on falsely made claims of abuse.

I honestly believe this generation is more manipulative than previous generations. They have no problem making something out of nothing. Many could easily be coined drama mongers. In previous times adults could say whatever to a child and there wouldn't be any backtalk; not that everything that was stated to a child was in their best interest. However, nowadays the law is a phone call away for our youth for the simplest of things. The old ways of discipline simply do not work anymore.

In order to find the lost kings and queens we have to play chess not checkers. The game of checkers will cause an individual to react on impulse rather than making a decision based on sound judgment. As a parent or guardian, you want to be able to do both without looking like the bad guy. We've all heard the old saying "you catch more bees with honey" and that is so true. Don't criticize out of spite and don't discipline at a level 10 with the expectation of a child responding at a level 3. Today's youth want structure and discipline, but we have to change the method of how we do it. I didn't say what we do, but how we do it.

Criticize With Love

Many parents may admit that if given a second chance, they would have made a better decision choosing a partner to raise a child with. Some of these parents have never moved past that decision, and it is the child that suffers. Therefore anger, resentment, and bitterness are behind their criticism of their child. That should never be, no matter what. A child does not ask to be created. It is the responsibility of a parent or guardian to make sure every word is edifying and not terrifying to the child. There are some who parent with an authoritative mindset—it's my way or the highway. Everything they critique is based on their perspective. That is very unfair to the teen because the world has changed; teens are dealing with more peer pressure now than ever.

Don't critique everything based on how you feel as a parent, look at it from their point of view. Give them the opportunity to feel their way through their problems. Let them make their own mistakes and figure out the answer on their own. It's so funny when people become parents and they believe that they now have a PHD in decision making. So parents or guardians when you do criticize, use a little love behind your judgment, even when you know they're wrong. There's nothing wrong with kids forming a thought process based on a situation. If you have done your job as a parent, your criticism will be a form of love instead of a striking force that causes pain.

If you have done your job as a parent, your criticism will be a form of love instead of a striking force that causes pain.

Whether you believe it or not, some parents are envious of their own kids. Why? Most of today's kids are more empowered than they were themselves. They get by with far more and there seems to be fewer repercussions for their actions. Yet they continue to look the other way. Parenting methods are either a direct or total opposite reflection of how a parent was raised. If they were raised in a strict home, they either parent the same, or they're overly permissive because they swore they would never be like their own parent. When the child ages and the parent see that the permissive method is not working and their child is running amok, they try to switch it up. But they find it difficult, if not impossible to bring the child back on track.

A fear parents often have is that their child will repeat the same mistakes they made. Because of this they do everything they possibly can to prevent this. Some may smother the child to where, like any trapped person, they are going to find a way to break out. This escape is done in an outrageous manner. A parents' self-resentment for their own choices can often come out as criticisms to their child, from everything their child does or to the people with whom their child associates. The parent is on constant alert, looking for signs of their own behaviors potentially being repeated. But these behaviors are imagined in the mind of some parents. This is called situational criticism.

People who criticize negatively base this on their situation. Their beliefs are that because it happened to them, it may happen to their kid(s). In their mind they are helping. But helping is not hurting. Don't criticize with hurt as a parent. Let love direct you and patience guide you as a parent. So many teens dislike their parents because of the negative criticism and pessimistic attitude they have about life in general.

L O V E conquers all. In my years of mentoring, speaking, and developing youth this has been my experience. No matter their gender, I have never had an issue with disrespect or inattentiveness because even my criticism is done with love. I do not tell them how they should do it, but instead I suggest why they should do it a different way. My method helps teens to consider the pros and cons of their actions. No matter who you are critiquing, it always needs to be delivered with a positive and uplifting tone. It is inevitable that parents will criticize out of frustration which leads to anger, and in return anger leads to the action of saying something that can't be taken back. Critiquing with an open mind is essential. Critique to build, not tear down.

Love will unlock any door of frustration because you can't fight fire with fire. We all must know how to diffuse something that can grow from small to enormous. The best strategy to use for a child that is sensitive as opposed to a child who can take constructive criticism is simple; change your approach. If we can choose our words and operate in a positive manner, we will receive a better response.

Discipline With A Purpose

Mississippi is one of the few states that still allows corporal punishment by a teacher. Many other states differ depending on the discipline tool or action that was taken toward the child. This is a slippery slope, because no one will ever know what really happened except the people who are present. Disciplining in the school has become a main attraction for a lawsuit. What are the parents or teachers to do? Most parents believe their hands are tied by the law when it comes to disciplining their own child. It's just like anything else people overly use, and it becomes abuse. The courts have seen their fair share of parents inflicting pain out of their own pain or because they can. This is not supported in any way.

Disciplining with a purpose provides a parent and the child with an understanding of the actions being taken. Then you will have set a foundation for that child to follow. My observations come from working with teens who have had a parent to discipline out of frustration. Many times I have heard students say that their parent just started hitting them without explaining. It made me think of my mother's famous line "I am whipping you because I love you." My reply was, I didn't know love could hurt so bad.

My parents had a purpose when they disciplined us. My father would say, "I'm not going to whip you for nothing unless you did something wrong." Younger parents are confused because they are kids raising kids. We have a large population of parents who are out of touch with this current generation of youth. Many don't have a clue when it comes to this new age of teens. The parents are not explaining the whys. I understand that the parent feels they are authorized to control their home as they should. As a parent, give the reasons behind what you say and do so there can be understanding.

When a child has an understanding, it gives them clarity into the reason for the disciplinary action. But if that is neglected because the parent feels it's their house, lights, food, and right to discipline, then there may be a backlash.

As always, it is important to understand the times. No neighbor should discipline a child and send them home. Why? One too many times and little Debbie comes home with bruises and marks. Guess what? That family is a million dollars richer. What once was "it takes a village to raise a child" is now a very risky venture. The village now has its limitations, leaving many parents left on a deserted island. Even teachers have been placed under supervision when it comes to discipline.

Let's reflect back on the game of chess again for a minute. In order to build rapport with your child, I know this may sound crazy, but a parent or guardian has to use strategy. Instead of using a belt or the first thing in sight, discipline with the thing they love. For an example, shut down all Wi-Fi, stop purchasing the brand name shoes they have to have, and refuse to pay for haircuts and nails.

The one thing parents have to get under control is disciplining while they are at their boiling point. This is never a good choice. I totally get when you are angry at another person, young or old, sometimes it is hard to hold back and wait till you have calmed down before you address the issue, but we must! Anger can take anyone to a place they didn't know existed. Standing on the outside looking in, it is very hard to be a parent because there is not an instruction manual. The primary goal is to deal with each child as an individual and to parent accordingly. One thing I believe is that parents need to stand by their principles and values. Never compromise them as a parent, but make sure they are still relevant. If not, please consider different methods.

Stop Blaming Schools

There are about 19 states where corporal punishment is legal in the school systems. However, mothers are not fond of their child getting paddled. Then of course, if it does happen, many are quick to file lawsuits. It is my opinion that discipline in school would not even be needed if parents were doing their job. It actually turns my stomach, because teachers are not responsible for doing the job of a parent. That is parenting; I stand by my statement as a mentor toward parents. Your child is a reflection of what you say and do in front of them. Parents need to stop pointing the finger at the schools and take responsibility for their children.

A parent cannot expect a teacher to articulate their lesson plans and teach basic manners at the same time to about 30 students. Come on, the school is for the advancement of a child's education; home is for the advancement of the character of that child. What a school does is display the sum of what is being instilled in the child at the home. If a parent doesn't want to be misrepresented, then they need to change what they are presenting to their child.

This is not said to be insensitive, but are just my thoughts. And if you find offense to it, you may want to take a better look at your parenting. What if the parents of some of these children that have terrorized schools and even taken the lives of innocent people, had been more responsible in their parental duties? How would things have been different? We have allowed society to raise our kids with television, video games, and entertainment; but when it comes to a tragedy we quickly blame the schools.

I most certainly disagree that the schools are at fault for these catastrophic school events. We have taken prayer out of the schools, only for it to be replaced with metal detectors. We remove teacher's assistants leaving 30 to 40 plus students under the guidance of one adult in a classroom. We have cut funding for education and we display little support to the future of our youth, which are the lost kings and queens. These teens notice this activity, and once again when criticism or discipline takes place, it causes a chain reaction. This chain reaction will affect not only the child, but has the potential to span out to their fellow classmates, friends, and educators.

We have taken prayer out of the schools, only for it to be replaced with metal detectors.

Our teachers' hands are tied; a teacher cannot break up a fight or openly correct a student. We have become a soft society and no one is really winning! A teacher's compensation does not nearly reflect the amount of hard work and time that is invested by dedicated teachers for the betterment of their students. We can all use the excuse that it is their chosen profession. But shouldn't we value our educators of tomorrow's leaders more?

The bottom line is that parenting starts at home as does respect. If we are not parenting, where do we get the right to blame anyone else for our own shortcomings? We all can adapt different methods and approaches when it comes to parenting our future leaders. It can start as simple as using our words wisely; thinking before we open our mouths. Use words that draw them in and not push them away. With the direction our youth are taking, if we don't change our behavior, we are in serious trouble. If the parents hands are tied, and the teachers are incriminated, who is left to direct and guide our teens?

Chapter 12
Perception vs. Reality

There is a huge difference between having a mental image as opposed to the state of being real. What is not can't be measured to what is. Our society has built its standards on perception and creating a fairy tale image in a real world. By doing so, we have lost the basic foundation on education, honesty in business, and our self-respect in general. We have become a nation that is hungry for materialistic possessions. Intelligence is viewed as overrated in the American culture.

As a society, we are lacking when it comes to providing our youth with ample excellent role models based on intelligence rather than stardom or material possessions. We have more access to stars than ever, making it easier to follow and monitor every move they make. If there is a teen that has no positive role models, it's more likely they will follow the path of what's hot in social media or amongst their peers.

It is crazy that very few people are happy being themselves. Everyone dreams of a make believe life that does not exist. I am so sorry but fairy tales just aren't real. They are a bunch of tales that we think make us feel good. There is no such thing. The tragedy of it all is our teen's inability to differentiate between the two. Many adults can't make that differentiation either. Our society has created a perception that not even they believe is real. In the real world when someone is shot, they don't get up and walk away.

When someone commits a crime for the world to see on a viral video, there are real consequences for their actions. Unfortunately, it is the crime that is glorified rather than the consequences. Television and music have the loudest voice, because they have the power to form and create in the mind of the youth.

Entertainment builds this platform that kids think they want to perform on, until he or she realizes the audience is brutal. Our youth don't know that there is no quick way to success; there are only a few web sensations that ever get noticed. There is only one Justin Beiber, Soulja Boy, Tyrese Gibson just to list a few of what seem like overnight stardom, but even for them it took work, dedication, and the consistency in their efforts to be better than good.

The perception is that all you have to do is be good and you can make it; if that was reality then anyone who is remotely talented would be a millionaire. To be perfectly honest, being good is to be expected. It's the norm. Being good is simply just waking up and doing the bare minimum. Fact is, in order to excel beyond belief it takes more than being just good—you need to be excellent and you need to be in demand. Even excellence alone at something doesn't mean you will become rich or famous. Perception can form a false pretense.

Only a few search beneath the surface of the lies, and realize that no one can party all week and succeed in the work place. It's funny how the media displays people sitting in coffee shops talking and never going to work. If we are not careful, our perception of reality can easily be altered.

I have heard this on several occasions "Perception is reality." I totally disagree, because a perception is based on what is formulated in the mind of an individual. From how we raise our kids to how we operate in relationships, a lot of us reside on a fantasy island that has drifted into the middle of nowhere. It is our job to create a real perspective for our teens, which will prepare them for the real world, life, and success.

Behind The Curtains

I was well into my childhood before I realized that Sesame Street was operated by people walking and talking through the puppets. Before that, no one could tell me that Bert and Ernie were not real characters, up until the day the curtain fell. I remember it like it was yesterday; the characters were guests on a morning talk show. During the segment one of the characters fell from behind the couch and I saw a hand come up and the character started talking again.

I was in disarray. What I had thought were real characters were merely puppets being operated by someone's hand. How many times do we read someone's profile only to find out that they're not who they portray? There is a big problem on social media of people pretending to bigger than life, when it's not their reality. It is easy to do because there is no real personal interaction so it creates the perfect environment for those to live the life they wish they had, but in fact do not. Not that they couldn't, but it is easier for them to portray being big online than it is to achieve it in real life. This is an epidemic affecting our youth. They have lost sight of what is real, and share far too much. They can create a virtual world of what they want to believe exists, and build their value off of status likes, comments, and friend counts.

What have we done? Young boys post pictures of marijuana and stacks of money, talking about how they get money, creating the perception they have it going on but in reality giving the impression they are selling dope. Some may be, but others are "fronting." Why would anyone feel it was a cool thing to front as a dope dealer? It is a sad display because most can't even form a coherent thought or even spell.

Since when did being a killer or crook become the hottest thing?

The pressure of this false concept of wealth through drugs so highly praised through music persuades the youth to become stars in a virtual world. Teens don't realize that most of these posts are monitored by law enforcement daily because of such activity. Teens are idolizing rappers as glorified gangsters in the studio, but behind the curtains they are nothing like they their lyrics. But when the music is played, they are killers and crooks. Since when did being a hustler or dope boy become the hottest thing? What they don't know that jail or death wait for them behind this curtain.

Our girls have lost R E S P E C T for themselves. It is perceived that being a bad bitch has nothing to do with having an education. The word "Bitch" is a term of endearment used to address friends in today's society. Some women have become numb to the phrase because it's used so often. Some have adopted the meaning as their way of attracting the man they want. I grew up in the Delta of Mississippi, where you would hear the term "the way to a man's heart is through his stomach." Nowadays, that saying has changed to "the way to a man's heart is through your body" yet it couldn't be any further from the truth. But they believe it and prove it daily by posting sexual exploits and what they are willing to do. Why work a job? Money or (bands) will make a weak individual do whatever. Society gives the most attention to whoever wears the least clothing. Nothing is discreet, anything goes. If someone is not mentally tough they will find themselves parading their body to receive validation. This is what we display to our children.

Why is this? This is a perception that is created for them, and some have adopted it for themselves. However, when the curtain falls, and it will, they are left with years of disrespect, a past that will haunt them, pregnancies, and a high potential for sexually transmitted diseases, if not worse.

But we celebrate the drama. We are a sick and twisted culture. We complain about the issues teens face, but look at what we accept and allow. How is it that teen pregnancy is popular now? What constitutes shows like *16 and Pregnant* as a hit while exploiting these teens that don't have a clue about rearing a baby. They don't care because we watch it; the ratings increase daily with our requests to keep up. Who reaps the benefits of this? The networks! Who loses? Our youth! How is that positive in any way?

Now, we have a little girl that feels insignificant and she is looking for affirmation. After watching that show she feels her only way out or to achieve some type of notoriety is to get pregnant at 16 (or younger nowadays even gets you more media attention) with the thought maybe she can get on TV and become famous. In hindsight, she doesn't know that behind the curtain, whether she is on television or not, the baby is her legal responsibility for the next 18 years.

All of these foolish perceptions that have been created are ruining our youth, and we must find our lost before it is too late. Our time is ticking fast due to the rapid increase of technology and the need for instant gratification. We chase money, cars, clothes and we are obsessed with this one word—SUCCESS. So many of our teens have a false meaning of success due to how the image was created in their mind. This has to change!

The Reality About Image

An *image* is a representation of a person, animal, or a thing. For the record, I am not writing to animals or a thing so this is addressed to people. Image is overlooked because of a false perception that is interpreted by an individual. The most important of all is your image. The reality about a person's image is based upon how they feel about themselves. The only way our children can build a positive self-image is if we change what they are observing. When your perception is built on what people tell you and not what you know, the spoken word overrides the inner belief, especially in the young.

Any one of us can become a confused individual, the minds of our youth are even more fragile to persuasion. They are open and vulnerable to any and everything like a sponge. The average teen is confused by what they hear and see. Their perception becomes the image they create based on society's standards, which are built on lies and deceit. If you don't know the wolf can wear sheep's clothing, you can never be aware of the possibility of a wolf in disguise. That is the trick of the enemy which is to keep the veil over the eyes as long as he can.

It is important for our teens to know their image speaks louder than words. Unfortunately, the value that was once placed on our youth no longer exists. They are not seen as the productive future members of society that they once were. My guess is many adults tend to think they are going to live forever, a mentality many share. As they strive for stardom and fame, and they chase the wind. Reality knows it is not easily attained. It takes hard work, but perception will show them it happens overnight. Perception tells them going to jail will sell more albums, not realizing the image they're creating.

When there is negativity involved, the image that is portrayed will be negative. Your image is exactly what others see and believe to be true as well. The bible says it best: "For as man thinketh, so is he." Thoughts govern your actions. People will see you for how you represent yourself. Many of our teens don't feel their inner value and represent that feeling in their actions. We have to get away from this bad boy/ bad girl image that our teens are taking on.

The glorified images of our culture, in general, have been downgraded to almost nothing. Our standards are below normal, even the image of being educated is diminishing. We have lost our edge as parents, educators, and guardians to the fascination of having "SWAG." Image is not in your clothes or shoes, it's who you are inside. We must get a move on our youth's image. From sagging pants to tattoos on their necks, the value of an image is a stock that is dropping daily. The responsibility is ours, but the accountability is theirs to keep. At the end of the day, their image will be the sum of their thoughts. But their thoughts will be the product of what we present to them.

Perception or Reality?

Chapter 13
The Challenge

There are many different meanings for the word "chal-lenge," it can be a confrontation or a call to action. I am challenging you in asking that you accept this call to action. I want to take the opportunity to call upon every reader in a position to influence a young king or queen's life. The power that you hold is more powerful than you will ever know. In the scheme of things, we as parents, educators, and mentors are the bow and the youth is the arrow. They will go in the direction that we point and shoot them towards; therefore we are in a position to cause change.

When I heard the news that my parents were getting a divorce, I was crushed. I was in middle school when my fa-ther started becoming absent on Fridays only to return on Sundays for church as if nothing was wrong. It angered me that he was sleeping in the other room and my mother had her king size bed by herself grasping for answers. I sat in the pulpit Sunday after Sunday knowing that my family was far from perfect. But the image we projected to everyone was that everything was ok. But I grew tired of hiding the lies.

I began acting out in the 8th grade hanging out with the wrong crowd. I even claimed to be a gangster disciple at one time looking for acceptance. Disobeying my father was the norm; I no longer respected the man of the cloth, because the cloth had more holes than a clarinet.

It's commonly said that preacher's kids are the worst, a stigma I was living up to. I was the worst and I did not care about it. I disrupted class looking for attention because my daddy was not at my football games. He was at church. My teacher couldn't control my anger. I felt invincible because I wanted everyone to pay for what my mom and my family was going through. To make matters worse, we lived in a small town in Mississippi where everyone knew your business and it seemed as if my family was the joke of the day every day.

I acted out due to my feelings being hurt. I couldn't change the way things were in my family. No one asked me what was wrong or seemed to even care. The teachers said I was hanging around the wrong type of kids but it was really what was going on behind the scenes at home that drove me to act this way. This forced me to carry out a plan to destroy and disrupt. In my mind, at least I was being heard. Driven by pain, I began to hate my father for the embarrassment.

Yeah, I was 13, and many thought I was just a kid, but I knew more than what people gave me credit for. Just like so many instances today, parents believe that their kids don't know what is going on. Take note parents, kids know more than you assume. I encourage all parents to observe and ask questions. It may not affect you, the parent, but the child may be silently suffering. I began praying for God to remove us from the situation only to see my mother in a better place.

In 1996, my mother loaded up a U-Haul truck with her furniture and 3 kids and walked away from a 15 year marriage. In the process, we heard that my father remarried and fathered 3 other kids. Wow. Talk about a blow to the gut. Now, I had the responsibility of being the man of the house and taking care of things. Listening to my sisters cry everyday about how they missed our dad only drove me to a deeper level of hate. Because I could not make their pain go away, I quickly filled the shoes of uplifting and motivating the 3 women who became my biggest fans on Friday nights. Their support drove me through high school. Even when I wanted to uproot and run for the hills, I couldn't because they looked to me for strength.

I became a father to my sisters teaching them how to play basketball and helping them with their homework while being a stand in husband by cooking, cleaning, and comforting my mom. I stood back and watched my mother, forced to carry on alone, working manual labor jobs to support us, after spending 15 years with a partner. At night my eyes would drown in tears asking why my family? The pain was spreading like cancer into my language, thoughts, body, and my behavior. On the outside I was fighting hard to stay strong for "Jay's Angels," a name I gave my mother and sisters.

My mother became my rock. I knew she only had a high school education and that being a pastor's wife was her only mastered profession. Peeping into her room, watching and listening to my mama on bent knees asking God to help her, drove me to become Mr. Fix it. So, I buried myself in the family genes. Football became everything because I could deliver hits that would inflict the pain I felt and I would go to college and then to the pros.

Coaches and teachers tend to have more of an influence on students than any other authority figures. They provide a strong support system because of the level of respect given to them by athletes. The only problem is that when school or the game is over, reality sets in when the child returns home. Coach Dave Sammons, Coach Andy Modica, and Coach Roger Benefield kept me on track and made sure that I went to class. But, when I walked through the door at home, reality would hit again.

All of my plans would change when my mom remarried the man I would grow to hate from a distance. Now my journey starts. The step-dad from hell was related to Lucifer be-

cause he was a great manipulator. The distant hate was so extreme that I contemplated suicide as a refreshing answer. I hated the nightmare I woke up to daily. I grew tired of his rants and the controlling acts of Hitler. Death became the answer to everything; whenever my step-dad would anger me it resulted in me thinking of killing myself.

I began reaching out to a teammate who later became my best friend. Andrew Marr began inviting me over to his home and I began talking about my home life. Woody and Shirley learned of my story and they took on the challenge of investing in me. They invited me into their home and treated me as if I was one of their own sons. Shirley often questioned me about college and my plans after graduation. I had no idea how to fill out a college application or that I could get a scholarship playing football. The Marr family became my home away from home; it was there I would see that I wanted more out of life than what I saw at home. A white family took a little confused, hurt, broken African American boy into their lives and home. It was unusual for me at the time coming from Mississippi, but I embraced the challenge and the exposure to even greater possibilities. I would bounce back and forth between the Marr's house and my home. I missed my mother often, but I knew I couldn't change her decision of marriage and reveled in the new things I was being exposed to at the Marr's.

Some would say this was a typical story in a suburban sports town, but this family saw something I definitely didn't. They took the challenge that so many run from because I was not their child. I saw how the Marr's were living and how they had dinner as a family. Mr. Marr was so active in his son's life. I coveted that feeling so badly. I never wanted to go home. I stayed with the Marr family most of my junior and senior year. Between my mom telling me that I was going to be great and Mrs. Marr telling me I was going to college, I felt I couldn't lose and the world was at my command.

Well, into college I went. There was no Marr family and my mother had become homeless. Here we go again, is what I said. My mama and sisters spent their lives now living on someone's living room floor, to a motel while my mom steadily searched for a place for her and my sisters. Mr. Fix it was at it again, wanting to quit college and return home to help.

My plan to go home was blocked by my coach. He challenged me to stay and not to go home with the most insolent tone. I had a choice to make, either punch him for not empathizing with my situation or drink my tears and stay because the NFL was on the path along with my degree. I dedicated my mind, body, and soul, to the game of football. I loved something that ended up never loving me back. After finishing my collegiate career and preparing for the NFL draft, I had two cousins and an uncle in the pros and not one of them reached out to me. There I was, standing alone.

On the seat watching the draft, all fell through the cracks leaving me still sitting alone. Several teams called about a free agent deal but not one sent papers. I chased the dream of playing professional football and changing my mother's life for good. I wanted to repay her for all of the hurt, pain, and loss she experienced. My last opportunity came when the Green Bay Packers flew me up for a workout.

I thought I performed well, as usual, as it was in my blood. Yet on this day they would feel that someone else was better because of his experience. Standing on the outside looking in, waiting for an opportunity to come that never would. After I was called and they said that they were going in a different direction, I knew it was over. The chase was over and I was out of breath, I could no longer run behind the love of my life.

A year later, I found myself sitting on the bedroom floor in my girlfriend's apartment with a knife to my wrist. I began cutting myself and stabbing the knife into my arm as tears streamed down my face, ready to end my life. I was left alone with my thoughts, fears, and the pain that had haunted me all of my life. I never knew that the divorce of my parents would have affected me so much, but it did. My inability to cope with pain and anger had gotten the best of me. Football became everything. And when football failed, I crumbled.

I thought that if I made it to the Pro's, my daddy would be proud of me and he could see me become something without his input. My pursuit of the NFL was not about the money. It was a coping mechanism, because I was able to express my pain, and I could give vengeance to my opponent without any consequences for my actions. I could hide behind the helmet and cradle myself in my pads and no one would know the demons I was fighting and the pain I was feeling on the inside.

I know for a fact that so many athletes bury themselves in workouts and playbooks just to cope with life. So many of us put all of our eggs in one basket, like I did with football, because we believe that participating in sports is a quick way to fix all of our problems. There are many young boys who are filling the roles of their fathers in their homes. And when sports or another dream fail, they are lost and forgotten. They can't seem to find that same acceptance and voice they once had on the field, court, or the diamond. I personally feel there are many athletes who are left in the dark, because no one takes the challenge beyond the sport. The challenge is never ending. There are so many men and women who are having difficulty coping with life because they have never coped with their past.

Now, I have taken the challenge to take my message worldwide to find our youth, the lost kings and queens. I have chosen to go into the churches, schools, and neighborhoods.

I am in pursuit to find them. Athletes, non-athletes, geeks, black sheeps, goth, rich, poor, gay, black, white, Asian, Hispanic, whatever, it doesn't matter, I want them all. I am challenging myself daily to find them because no matter what, they deserve to wear their crown. It took me over 15 years to discover I was born to rule, and that I AM A KING.

I have vowed to be transparent about all of the different phases of my life. Whether it is sports, identity issues, depression, suicide, looking for love and wanting validation from my father—the good, bad and the very ugly. I didn't know at the time of my journey why I had all these pot holes, and detours. Now I know it wasn't for me, it was for these lost kings and queens. I ask that you join me in finding our lost youth; it could be your very own child that is lost right under your nose. Don't assume that a kid is ok, ask questions, and be inquisitive in a strategic way. Insight will be retrieved when the questions are presented in the right way.

My Challenge To Men

Many times as men, we get caught up in a trap chasing success, and aspiring to get our cars, house etc. We develop tunnel vision and tend not to see anyone or anything around us because all of our focus is on other things. Nevertheless, we have always been kings to God; he granted Adam authority over all the animals in the garden. Adam had the power to name all the living creatures from dogs, cats, lions, tigers and of course the bear. He also possessed the power to call what God said was a helper; Adam called her a woman, Eve. Therefore we all have the same power to call and name the future kings around us.

Instead of calling them thugs, call them doctor, lawyer, electrician, and teacher.

In B.C. times, the men were in charge of naming the child, because whatever a man named a child carried the vision for the life of that child. Take control of your neighborhood and cities by picking up a king that is lost. Give them a title of honor.

In America today, 50 percent of marriages will end in divorce. Sadly, more than a few young boys will grow up without a father or male figure in their life. Our work is cut out for us men. We are the head of the household regardless of what society says. It starts with the man, life cannot be created without a man's participation. Every young man needs a male influence in his life to help guide him into manhood and not just learning how to use his tool.

True mentorship starts with being open and honest about the challenges of being a man. There is no easy button for a man. The world tells us not to cry and to suck it up. If a man expresses emotions he is considered weak, so I understand, we have been trained to keep quiet. But now is the time to break the silence—break that stereotype that feeling and having emotions is weak. Feeling and having emotions means only one thing—YOU ARE ALIVE!

Feeling and having emotions means only one thing— YOU ARE ALIVE!

We must help our muted suffering youth break their silence, by changing their view of what has become the norm by the media. The media doesn't care that suicide is steadily climbing among our young male population—in fact, the more out of control, the better their ratings. They don't care that 71 percent of kids without a father are more likely to drop out of school or that 90 percent of all homeless and runaway children are kids that had no dad at home (*The Fatherless Generation*).

The fact of the matter is that males matter, contrary to popular opinion. Men are needed. Whether biologically or as a step-father, they are needed. A man's presence alone says more than words. Even if you're not a vocal leader, be an emotional source of support. The streets are raising our young boys, and we all know the streets have their own sets of rules. I don't care how gangster, hood, or ghetto anyone feels they are, the streets are undefeated.

We are losing boys daily in innocent blood because no one wants to take the challenge. We must give our young boys hope in their hopeless situations. Shed some light by speaking and asking them how is it going? Is everything ok? These are just a few questions you can start with. Men we must start somewhere, what better place to start than in your local community. I challenge you to use these following principles to help find our youth.

Principles

- Be responsible and be a man of your words
- Hold them, and yourself, accountable
- Be determined to see the youth do better
- Be driven
- Create a desire to implement change
- Maintain a great work ethic
- Remember success is a process
- Never abort your mission as a Man
- Value yourself as A King
- One must have a foundation in God for any of these to work, or teach them
- A true king has a foundation in God

It's great to be successful in life and obtain all of the things we dream about. How about giving someone else the opportunity to dream and live out their greatest desire? Push all ego and pride aside and embrace the life of another. In order for a King to hand over his kingdom, a young lad has to be trained, prepared to rule, and succeed the present king. The sad thing is that many of us can't hand over our kingdom because we don't have a successor.

Most have never reached back and pulled up one another. We've bought into this laid back, passive, not my problem mentality. It is our problem. Just think about this; if you have a daughter, what can she look forward to if no one reaches back to pull the sons up and help develop them into kings?

So this is bigger than all of us. The harvest is plentiful but the laborers are few. This is not a color issue; this is a global matter with our youth. Hip-hop has moved across all barriers, and for us to be relevant in today's generation, we must crossover into the inner cities, suburbs, urban, low income, high income, and yes, even the rural farmlands. Expose the young men to something different, because if we don't, they will never know that they were meant to rule. I will leave you with this gentlemen, a man that does not know he was born to rule, will be a servant forever.

"Until you know your ability to become great, you can never exercise your resources to do so."

Jay Barnett

My Challenge To Women

There was a time when women couldn't vote and touching the glass ceiling was unobtainable. Times have changed for the American woman. Today she is the CEO of Sam's Club,

US Ambassadors to different countries, and coaches of World Cup teams. These are just a few of the entities of the work place which women would have never been considered decades ago. And yet, when I turn on my television I see Real Housewives, Teen Mom, and Basketball Wives. These entities are looked upon by our young teen girls as stellar careers— easier to achieve in their eyes than a CEO title. This has to be a joke and it's time to change the punch line. Young girls glorify drama up to the point of exploitation of one another on social media. The sad thing is that they are only repeating what they see their role models do, with some even being their very own mothers. We've all heard the saying monkey see, monkey do; I would never compare anyone to a monkey, but there is wisdom in the cliché.

Girls mirror what they see, similar as boys to men. These celebrated reality stars have become an influence on our young women today. Many of them are raising kids, while only a kid themselves. Most girls that have become a teen mom have only carried on the cycle of their own mothers. The only way the actions of anyone can be changed is if they see something different. I know from being raised by a single mother and the brother to two sisters that women can carry a lot of power.

If these women can step out of their independent roles for just a second, they will see that little girl that is searching through magazines looking for her identity trying to find her self-esteem amongst the pages. In fact, women and men deal with similar issues, just in different facets of life. Men have self-esteem issues that result in a poor self-image. Women have self-image issues that result in low-esteem. None of us are exempt from dealing with the battles of life while on the journey to become a man or woman. But we can help change the direction of a struggling youth.

Some women have trust issues because of their past experiences with their dad, uncle, or someone who may have taken advantage of them. These issues can make it hard for them to relate to men in the future. There is a lot of emotional building that goes into working with young ladies, so I encourage women to form groups that will empower one another to confront those issues.

Take a stand against the garbage that is portrayed about women and how the only way to the top is on your back or by marrying some athlete. Especially those who are single moms, I empathize with you. I commend and congratulate you for a job well done, for it is not easy raising kids by yourself. It takes guts, willpower, and the heart to wear the pants and the skirt. It is not easy on single mothers to play the role of a father and mother. I know some women are a little fed up with men, but if you can take the challenge to mother a daughter that is not yours, whether she has a male influence or not, you both will be better for it.

If television is going to continue to convey the message of women parading their bodies for the next big star, we're going to continue down the path of no self-respect. Women, enough is enough. Far too long you been overlooked, disrespected, and mistreated. Teach and train young ladies how to be queens over their mind, body, and soul without selling their soul. Their integrity is theirs to keep along with a sound mind and a pure body. Take back your rightful throne and change how women are viewed. They should only be viewed as smart, nurturing, intelligent, and caring. Instead, too many are being viewed as easy, disposable, and as an object to be used.

I remember what my mom was to my sisters. It hurt me so many times that my sisters had my mom to pattern themselves after and I had no one. My mother was a woman of great character. She didn't have a lot of female friends and she didn't gossip about other women. She taught my sisters that they had to carry themselves in excellence and to be in control of their decisions based on wisdom, not emotions. My sisters became what my mom was to them, an excellent mother and wife.

Her heart is goal oriented and made of pure gold; her mission is for others to succeed.

Women you can change the deception in the mind of a young girl to the truth. The truth is not the makeup, the bag, or the shoes; it is what lies beneath, under the cover of material guise. It is what the woman sees beyond the mirror, and what she thinks of herself. Men treat women how women treat themselves. Be an example to young ladies, you can be sexy and classy but there is no value in being sexy and trashy; that comes at a cheap price and can be sold or auctioned to anyone. A real queen's value is in her character, not in her wallet.

A real queen's posture is worth more than money; she is respected by her movement which reflects how she feels about herself. The queen's body language lets people know that she is confident, yet humble. Real queens serve and give back to the people. Her heart is goal oriented and made of pure gold; her mission is for others to succeed.

Ladies, teach our young women the following principles that they will need to be successful as a queen.

Principles

- Empower our young women that an education is very important

- Teach our young queens to judge by character and not looks
- Help them to remember beauty does not equate to confidence
- Remind them *make up* does not make them
- Teach them how to present themselves as ladies
- Gossiping is a bad habit
- Teach them how to build other women
- Show them that intelligence is classy
- Envy and jealousy are an ugly disease
- Being a lady *is* being a "Bad Chic"

God has a queen's heart until her king arrives.

The Conclusion

After sitting in my room contemplating and soul searching my life, I questioned myself. What else did I bring to this world aside running a ball and making a tackle? God revealed to me my first passion as a kid, preaching like my dad. When I was growing up, I had always worked with the youth in my dad's church. Back then I thought my pulpit would be the church, but it changed when I got a revelation of what today's youth was facing. I reflected on the pain I had experienced in the past that I hated to talk about. But then it dawned on me. All the things I went through in my adolescent and young adult years, as well as the struggles as an athlete, had a purpose.

I remembered how I had no one most of the time to talk with and how it made me feel. It was that one person that came along at the right time that helped me realize I could be more. I shifted my focus on what I had in me and what I could do with that life experience. I knew God was telling me to be that person who lifts another. I realized my life journey was not about me and that I had to do something with the wisdom I had obtained through the process.

Then, The Men of Excellence and Women of Excellence project was birthed in 2011, but I sat on it for a year and did nothing with it. I had all of these ideas about working with teens, but I wanted to be different. In 2012 the plan came together from heaven above, and I began to move forward.

The ME/WE is a 5 week program designed to develop and produce future kings and queens. This is accomplished through journaling, teaching them how to communicate, recognizing areas of improvement, helping them to form and create positive visions for themselves. The final week of the program teaches them how to bring it all together and become successful, reminding them success is whatever they want it to be. It is not in a salary, car, house, degree, or any tangible material possession. Our children are becoming susceptible to drugs, victims of bullying, and experience sex at an early age. My heart and efforts are now focusing on them. I began The ME/WE at KIPP Academy in Houston, Texas and I am looking forward to expanding it across the country.

Success is life. Success is doing better than what an individual has previously seen. My message is powerful, relevant, moving, most of all it is needed for a world that has lost its identity. I have channeled all my energy and passion toward the lost youth of America by establishing programs in the local schools, churches, and outreach centers. My passion drives me toward fulfilling my purpose to give the youth vision and direction. I want them to understand and to know for a fact that they have value, that they're important, and our society needs them to be productive.

There is no such thing as a lost cause; you lose when you lose the cause to keep seeking for answers.

Acknowledgement To My Mother And Father

I began writing letters to my dad several years ago, and even though he didn't know how to communicate with me I kept reaching out to him. I understood that he could only do what he had seen done, and it wasn't his fault. We began conversing regularly and started to build a close relationship. I have forgiven him and moved forward, for I could no longer carry the anger, resentment, and bitterness toward him. Even with him being a man of the cloth he was still human. I had to realize I was mad at him for not being something that I myself couldn't be, which was perfect. I have grown to love him all over again and we have a very strong relationship to this day. He has been by my side throughout writing this book, and I am proud to say he is one of my biggest fans.

My dad travels with me on speaking occasions; the little boy that once looked for validation finally received it on his 30th birthday. The first time in my life I heard my father say he was proud of me; words could not explain the feeling of knowing that both my heavenly and earthly father are proud of me.

My mother is still that strong woman that drove a 20 foot truck to Texas. My mother is and always will be my Queen, best friend, and favorite all around girl in the whole world. Even after I marry, she will always remain my inspiration and will always have my heart. We talk every morning; she was the inspiration behind this book and the prayer warrior that kept my spirits up. Even through my suicide attempt and depression battles she never gave up on me. She always did and will continue to speak positive and uplifting words to me. I am blessed to receive random texts from her saying that I am her hero. What she doesn't know is that she was one of the reasons I chose to live. I did not want my mother to bury her only son.

I know I will be GREAT just as mama always said. This drives me every day to be better than good. I pray my mission changes one king and queen at a time. I hope my message will help someone realize they are a king or a queen.

"Until we know who we are, we will never be able to go where we belong." "We are royalty." Most of all, I trust that my work and dedication to finding our lost youth will outlive me. Rule with dignity, integrity, and love.

I am a King!

-King Jay

About the Author

J ay Barnett was raised down in the Delta in a small Mississippi town called Gunnison. He graduated from Tarleton State University with a Bachelor of Science degree. Long after his pursuit to the NFL, Jay turned to his childhood gift, speaking and empowering teens. Jay's vision has become a new found message for many teens and adults today. The I AM A KING & I AM A QUEEN movement has taken the community by storm.

Jay's passion is undeniablely his greatest asset. He began a 5 week self development program called TheMEproject. The program is geared toward teen boys and girls in the Houston, Texas area where he now resides. Jay's vision is to reach the world with his message of empowering teens to be Kings & Queens, and never servants to anything or anyone but God.

3/29/14

Made in the USA
San Bernardino, CA
20 March 2014